Claire

by

Kerry O'Sullivan

Title: Claire

Genre: Fiction

Author: Kerry O'Sullivan

ISBN 978-0-6459257-7-7

Copyright © Kerry O'Sullivan

All rights reserved

First Published 2024

CLAIRE

Chapter 1

Justin Abbott thought all was well with his marriage, as he and June had been spouses for eighteen years. Both were professionals. He was an eminent historian with a pressing need to research man's history, and she was an advocate who worked for a large law firm in Glasgow. They looked their parts; they were in their forties, he a tall, dark-headed, pleasant-faced man who had let his appearance slip. He was now a parody of an academic historian; haircut needed, clothes a bit disheveled, untidy, a one-track mind. She had maintained her image; she was an attractive, well-dressed, blond-haired woman with a zest for life. He was comfortable with the routines of their married life, but she was not. June walked into his untidy office this day, scowled at the mess, and said,

"Justin, I have been having an affair with Robert from work for the past two years, and I want a divorce as we are going to get married."

This stunned Justin. He stood and looked at her for a long time.

"Did you hear me?" she said.

He stood mute, then said,

"Could you say that again?"

"You heard me; see a lawyer. I have mine." With that, she turned on her heels and left.

Anger and blame welled within him.

After all I have done for her.
What have I done for her?
Nothing much.

He tried to rationalize the situation in his mind.

"Justin, I have tried to speak to you many times. You always had to finish something. I gave up on you years ago, and you were unaware. What else could I do?" she said.

"Now that I see it, will you give me one more chance?" he asked.

"No, no, no, you do not need a wife; you're absorbed in your work. It is over two years since we made love. You are not even aware of that, are you? You were a skilled and kind lover. As a man, you are quite a pleasant fellow; as a husband, you are hopeless. Give it up," she said.

Justin went to see a solicitor friend, Alistair Blare, who smiled when told of Justin's predicament.

"I am not laughing at you. I have known you for over two years and didn't know you had a wife. Find out who June's solicitors are, and I will ring them and amicably arrange things. There is no reason for expensive court proceedings," Alistair said.

So, Justin became a single man again. All this gave him one thing: deep depression. He tried to continue his work, but to no avail. The bottle became his best friend. He drank every day and was in a permanent alcoholic haze. This situation persisted for many months until he saw his doctor, Blair Docherty, a lifelong friend.

"Well, Justin, get your face out of all those research books. If I were doing all that, I, too, would be a depressed drunk. You need two things: a change of occupation and environment."

"I cannot do that; I have no other skills," Justin said.

"Listen, my man; if my memory serves me right, you were halfway through a law degree before you decided that was not for you. You then started training as a schoolteacher; you taught history and were the best history teacher in town. You loved it, all those fresh minds to fill with the contents of your copious brain. Go back to teaching until you sort yourself out. Find a position far away from Edinburgh and go into the smaller towns. They are desperate for teachers. There, you will find a new life."

Justin thought long and hard about what Blair said. He knew he was correct.

He went to see the department and lodged an application. They were ecstatic to have such an experienced teacher and eminent historian on their books. The department gave him a list of small towns in the north of Scotland that were seeking a jack-of-all-trades teacher specializing in history. He started his research in towns as far away from Edinburgh as possible. The farthest place on his list was a little village on the northeastern coast of Scotland named Wotan, a name of yesteryear inhabited by a clan called Wotan. Hours of research in his history books and conversing with his like-minded friends revealed they were a clan from southern Europe that settled in the Caledones thousands of years ago. His excitement was palpable.

"This isolated clan could be a link back to ancient man," he mused.

Justin knew, at the beginning of that millennium, there was scant crossbreeding among tribes. He could not contain himself; the excitement was too much. Here was a living experiment of all his theories on ancient man and their ties to ancient laws, not society's dictates.

He phoned Blair. "I have found a place that is perfect for my project; this could be the missing link to prove my thesis. It is as far as you can go northwest of Scotland. Wotan is its name."

"I know Wotan," Blair replied. "Joan Wotan, a young lady at the tennis club, was born there; she told me the most interesting history. It is a fascinating place, and she is a fascinating woman. I can arrange for you to meet her if you like?"

"Oh, yes, please," Justin replied.

Justin rang and met Miss Wotan at his office. A very attractive young woman, she was mid-twenties and as bright as an army button.

"Here is a copy of a thesis I completed at the end of my English degree. It is on the history of Wotan. I received a credit for this work. Not bad, aye," she said.

Justin perused the work, written in perfect copperplate script, not unlike pen and ink.

"You have an excellent hand, Joan. I imagine you received a credit for handwriting," his schoolteacher's mind surmised as he glanced at the thesis. "What do you say I make us a cup of coffee, as I would like to read your thesis now, and ask you some questions? I am researching the Wotans and their clan ways."

"Yes, go to it. I've got plenty of time all day, in fact. Black coffee:" Joan said.

Justin made home-brewed coffee for two, sat comfortably with Joan on the settee, and read the thesis.

"The Wotans are a small tribe from the North of Scotland. A long, long time ago, Scotland was not its name. It was a barren part of Britannica and the Wotans, a Celtic tribe, came from Gaul, where considerable upheaval forced them across the sea to Britannica. There, the most basic of instincts, survival, drove them inland.

Being without food, these people commandeered any food they saw, which meant, most times, other tribes' sheep flocks. Their tribe's size gave them the power to take whatever they pleased; still the locals tried to defeat and expel them. Fierce battles followed these encounters. Although they always won, these battles fractured the tribe, and small groups spread far and wide.

Under their leader, Gael, one group traveled and moved away from the attacking tribes. Many confrontations saw them forced to battle to escape these attacks. Over time, suspicion became the first reaction toward any group who crossed their path. Mistrust and skirmishes saw them, and the remnants of their appropriated flocks; driven to the farthermost northwestern corner of the land. Here, a nomadic life affronted them with the real prospect of extinction.

When they reached the land's end, they settled, as there was nowhere else to go. Here the land was subject to the wild weather and seas of the North Atlantic that ended their tempest on the cliffs bordering the landscape. The winters were long, cold, and unpredictable; summers were short and subject to occasional squalls that scudded over the sea.

At the end of the journey, Fate shone a light on them; they stumbled upon a gap in the sea cliffs; this was the only coastal break for many days of travel in any direction. A spur at this break, formed in the cliffs, was a buffer to the sea's prevailing pounding. It diverted the waves' direct impact; they crashed into the cliff walls opposite the spur. This gap was narrow at its entrance and ran inward for some distance. It branched into a small bay that travelled parallel to the coast before petering out on a gravel beach.

The cliffs on the bay's ocean side were tall and rocky; on the land side, the terrain was steep and fell away to the bay. The other side of the bay was meadowland that rose as it travelled toward the east. A small spring-fed creek ran back through the meadow and trickled into the bay. The area at the beach end, a depression, was weather protected by the sea cliffs. It had the blessing of deeper soil than the plains, hence a covering of flowering gorse and small trees.

They settled here, on the downslope halfway from the clifftop, with the bay below. If strangers approached, the elevation gave excellent viewing and a defendable position.

Their ingrained tribal instincts were still intact. Attack and kill all outsiders. They lived in sheepskin tepees at first, then settled into dry-stone huts built from the myriad stones on the cliffs' ocean edge. Their food was from the offspring of the stolen sheep herd, copious fish caught in the bay and around the sea cliffs, and some greens and root vegetables leached out of the deeper soils of the depression.

They isolated themselves from the outside world tribulations until the eighteenth century. Since then, various people would come to their corner of the world and suffer fierce attacks; these defeated remnants would limp out of their domain. The word spread; stay away.

Then, toward the end of the reign of Queen Victoria, two people arrived, messengers of God. A man and a woman dressed in black; the man held a small cross as a sign of peaceful intent. He was leading a donkey loaded with all their possessions. To Eilig, the tribal leader, it was clear their intentions were benign; he and the elders met the interlopers on the plain. The man, a learned fellow, could understand their ancient Gaelic language; he conversed with them.

"My name is Sydney Tott; I am here with my wife, Maude, to spread the word of Our Lord Jesus Christ. We have many interesting things to share with you. Are we welcome?" he asked.

Eilig and the elders conferred and allowed the Totts to stay if they worked and contributed to the community. They were valuable contributors. As compensation, the locals helped them build shelters and settle in. There was much interest in their possessions, implements such as scissors, and their small quantity of carpenters' tools. Of fascination were their books with all the strange markings.

Through the Totts, reading and writing became part of everyone's skill set in the settlement. The Totts upgraded the community's Gaelic tones and pronunciations and brought them into modern times. Among the books the Totts brought were histories, storybooks, and books about Jesus. The people liked the biblical stories and complied with Totts' teachings.

Religion, a peaceful religion, had arrived in their midst. They accepted the Ten Commandments. Even "Thou shall not kill," although their interpretation of the commandment was "it applies within their tribe, not to outsiders." Sydney thought it wise to let their interpretation prevail.

The Totts lived among them for many years until Maude became sick and died. Maude's death devastated Sydney. He remained in the community until his death some years later, but he did not take part in village life. The village sympathized with him and cared for him to the end. Nobody came to replace him, and religion waned. Some people came, looked, and left. They were not interested in this godforsaken corner of the world. Except for one group, more messengers of God, the New Calvin Kirks of Scotland, their message was strictly New Calvinism. Here to them was a fertile field, a settlement with no competition. This religion did not give its flock a welcoming beginning; its first governing principle, humanity in every aspect, heart, emotions, will, mind, and body, carries the stain of sin. From that, one had to earn one's salvation.

A succession of ministers, all stern, black-garmented men, reminded them their future was fire and brimstone. Over the years, the Wotans became a religious group and built a small kirk on the hill that overlooked the settlement. The ministers had a word to say on everything in the settlement and woe betide those that ignored their religious leader's commands. Although all stayed true to the tribe and its ethos.

At the time of the First World War, Wotan entered the twentieth century. Officialdom had found them and brought electricity and a range of unwanted services, plus charges and taxation, to their community. Historians now had an interest in them. A new people in Scotland; impossible! Where did they come from? How long had they been here? They read and write?

They dug for the answers. Anecdotal history gave some. It was the contents of the ancient gravesites and the original houses' remains that gave the clues needed. Small metal objects from earlier times were the major clues. The consensus was that these people were Celts, from what is now Europe, and had remained hidden for many centuries. They found evidence from some five hundred years ago of a mass burial. The bodies' positions suggested that most had frozen to death and remained exposed for a lifetime before burial.

The mini-ice age, with its extreme cold, had frozen the ground solid, making it impossible to dig graves until much later. Another period of mass burial occurred in the eighteenth century. There is an oral history that tells of a sickness that came from shipwrecked sailors and killed most of the people. I suspect it would have been like the influenza virus that decimated the Native Americans when the Europeans arrived.

"That is quite a story. Can I have this copy?" Justin asked.

"Indeed, when you reach Wotan, your guide will introduce you to Edward and Shirley. Most visitors stay in their house. They will bring you up to date on all the pertinent happenings over the past few generations. He is a veritable chatterbox.

"Tell them you have heard the basic Wotan story from me," Joan said.

"They are a most helpful couple and are no friends of the current settlement hierarchy."

"What a fascinating story. Thanks for the contacts; they will be invaluable. All this has stoked my curiosity about Wotan. I cannot wait to get there. How can I thank you?" Justin's manner and disposition had lit the fires of attraction between them.

"Take me out for dinner tonight at the swankiest restaurant in town?" she asked.

Justin laughed. "Okay, you are on. You can pick the restaurant. Give me your address, and I will pick you up at seven."

Joan's invitation fascinated him.

She does not know if I am a married man; she does not care. Going out with me was foremost in her mind, so going out was what we would do. I do not know what will happen, but I intend to find out. A single-minded young woman, she knows what she wants, and she will get it.

He mulled over the whole situation. It excited him. Joan was a beautiful young lady.

Justin picked Joan up, and they took a taxi on a brief journey to the Cael Bruich Restaurant, which was very upmarket indeed. "A good choice," he mused.

Confident, Joan was a provocative conversationalist and exciting company. The most exciting moment was when, with a twinkle in her eyes, she said. "Now you can take me to my place, where we can make erotic love." This invitation floored him; the reply he mustered was a weak, "Of course."

In the morning, on his way home, he pondered on the night before.

What a character. If she represents ancient woman, they can rule my roost.

The next day, Justin went to the Education Department and accepted the position of history and geography teacher at Wotan Public School. As it was the end of the school year, the position was to begin in January.

In January, he contacted the school; they told him he would replace Mrs. Hobbs, who was a popular teacher.
"If she is so popular, why is she leaving?" he asked.
"She had a falling out with the Reverend."
What has a reverend to do with school teaching?
This incident worried him, and he did further research. New Calvin Kirks of England was their religion. It was a name that gave connotations of the Church of England, a staid and respectable institution. Research informed him how wrong he was; it was a minor institution with strict New Calvinistic Doctrine interpretations. He could now see how the minister could dominate village life. He looked long and hard at abandoning the posting; then guilt flooded him.

I don't like this; my vibes say, "don't go," but I must go. I have committed myself to the position, others are depending on me, and most of all, I need to finish my research. I will keep my head down, do what I must, and perform the job at hand. I will fulfil my twelve-month contract,"

In January, Justin took the train journey to Kinlochbervie as directed, and traveled to Wotan on the current boat, the *Esmeralda*. A trip he enjoyed, as he knew boats. Both his grandfather and father had owned boats. The sea was moderate, the powerful engines' strum and the hull's stability in the sea impressed him; *Esmeralda* had a steady and safe feel. Its conversion from deep-sea fishing trawler to ferry/trader comprised alterations on alterations, irrespective of the finished product. It was perfect for the job at hand.

He had contacted the Village Council and discovered it doubled as the Church Council, and met Ralph Wotan at the wharf. Ralph was late and kept Justin waiting. Justin was glad to have a little time to himself to examine his new surroundings. As he was standing on the wharf, the ship's captain, signified by his battered cap, stepped onto the

quay. He passed Justin with a smile and headed to the first of a row of cottages next to the store.
Ah-ha, the captain's abode.

He looked back at the store, which was the centre piece of the town and dominated the surroundings. It was a large two-story freestanding building clad in horizontal strips of timber boarding. They were now gray after many years of bleaching by the weather. Justin walked in, and a pleasant, middle-aged, greying woman greeted him.

"How can I help you?" she asked.

"Oh, I'm Justin Abbott, the new schoolteacher, and I am waiting for Ralph."

"Oh, good. I'm Beryl McNabb; you will teach our daughter, Felicity. As for that Ralph, he is always late. That man will be late for his funeral; here he comes now; I will let you go and serve my customers."

Ralph was an unsmiling, uncommunicative little man who mumbled a few words of greeting. Justin informed him that the next day at eleven he had an appointment with the school principal.

"Do not be late," Ralph said.

Ditto to you, old son.

The council had arranged a room with Edward and Shirley Wotan. The couple Joan had mentioned, a pair whose adult daughter—it happens with all the bright ones— had left the village and now lived in London.

Edward Wotan greeted him at the door and introduced his wife, Shirley.

"We received a note from young Joan, so we have been waiting for you, especially Shirley."

"Ha, what about you? You haven't been able to sit still for days, peeping through the front curtains every five minutes. Anyway, come in, and we will show you the room and fill you in on the past few generations of Wotans," Shirley said.

It was a pleasant house, and they offered him the attic room. He could see the meadow and the sheep from its small, attached bathroom. He liked the room, the house, and his landlords. They were a polite couple, excited about the new schoolteacher coming to stay. After dinner, Edward produced a valise, opened it, and brought out a handwritten document.

"This is the manuscript of a novel I was writing called *Wotan*. It was about our recent generations. I never completed it as the pinnacle of my writing ability was way below expectations."

"What he is saying is his talents hadn't improved since his primary schooling," Shirley said.

"Well, put it straight, as Shirley often does. I cannot write, but it is historically correct. It will give you a feel of the character and vibes of the settlement during the recent decades," Edward said.

"Edward, this will be more valuable to me than *The Complete Works of William Shakespeare*," Justin replied.

"Well, I am glad they are useful to someone."

"A stopped clock, at one moment, is right every day." As usual, Shirley had the last word.

Justin was eager to take his leave and return to his room. He cleared his desk and read.

As he wanted, the history, although poorly written as Shirley said, gave him further insight into the modern history of Wotan.

"What a fascinating history. What an exciting place this is! I can't wait to start my teaching career, but most of all, my research."

The hub of the town was the area on the shore of the bay where the *Esmeralda* birthed. Premises were in a row along the length of the shore, removed from the edge by the wharfing area that ran the entire length of the bay. The people of the town built up and paved the area with cobbles from the oceanfront. This was the town centre and the place of all town activities. It was a popular place for social promenading.

The school in the town was a typical two-level Education Department building, with classrooms on both levels. In this atmosphere, where the school community was under the Reverend's eagle eye jurisprudence, Claire completed her schooling. In the primary years, the lack of understanding of the surrounding happenings gave the little ones the bliss they needed. She enjoyed every day she spent there, either with her friends or in a class with Beryl McNabb, a loving and kind grandmother type. At the end of the year, Claire went to senior school under the auspices of Miss Johnas, who would be her teacher for the next two years. In her final years at the school, the children were fifteen and sixteen years old, and a new teacher, Miss Hobbs, was to replace Miss Johnas.

The Reverend had died of old age; they said. The kirk elders buried him in the Kirk grounds, and the New Calvin Kirks of Scotland sent a large man as the replacement, minister, the Right Reverend Samual Keith Godley, a black-garmented tyrant. On his first day, he called a meeting at the kirk that all men of the community must attend. In his eyes, women were subservient to their men. Threats were his first utterances. He informed the Kirk Council he would review their positions within one month, and those who received his approval would remain.

He also told the attendees he was the anointed messenger of God, and he decided who would be the elect of the congregation. The elect, and only the elect, would enter the Promised Land. As New Calvinistic, God-fearing people, the citizens of Wotan took these threats seriously. It became a very somber community. People worked, stayed indoors, and went to the kirk. Calamity befell any that did not attend kirk at the appointed times. From this point, the Sword of Damocles hung over every adult resident. Joan Hobbs was the feisty kind and knew all about the Reverend's style. After the Reverend's continuous interference with her class programs, frustration caused anger to rise within her, and she confronted him.

"I know your game, stay with your religion, and keep away from my classes. If you don't, I will have my brother involved so fast that it will take your breath away. You don't know him, do you? He is the editor-in-chief of the *Glasgow Herald*. He will do a complete background check on you; I would say that you have left a dirty trail. Be warned, stay out of my classes and away from my children." With that, the Reverend left.

At the end of the year, the council told Joan Hobbs they did not need her services at the school or town. As she came from Glasgow, she had no option but to return there.

At eleven sharp the next day, Justin reported to Oliver McGinty, a contemporary of the Reverend from Glasgow. McGinty was a dour fellow, mid-seventies, retirement age. He was a very polite and formal man who walked Justin around the school building. It was typical of smaller Education Department schools, upstairs and downstairs, with eight classrooms on each level, divided into four classrooms on each side by a hall down the middle. The school conducted coeducational classes for all ages, from six years old to sixteen years old. It taught the Education Department curriculum subjects, plus two independent subjects designed to reflect the local town and surroundings. Reverend Godley commandeered these two independent subjects for his preaching purposes. A walk across the school grounds saw them in a small building. It was Administration and the teachers' common room. Here he met the teachers, a typical group if ever there was one.

Many, on twelve-month Education Department contracts such as Justin, are not interested in the school or community gossip or politics. Their interest was in the extra money they earned for working at the end of the world and the town's lack of facilities to spend it; they were there to save money. And save money they did.

Chapter 2

It was one week till the beginning of the term, and Justin spent all his time preparing for his students.

When the day arrived, a rowdy crowd of students of all ages was in the yard below the classroom. Then a large man in black strode across the school grounds. There was silence in the vicinity preceding him. The children scattered and parted before him and closed after he passed, like a school of fish evading a predator. This fluctuating scene progressed across the school grounds. The cleric was unaware of the surrounding happenings.

What monster of a man do we have here? Stay away from me; I am not ready for you.

The Reverend did not stay away; he stomped up the stairs and strode right up to Justin, standing dumbfounded in the middle of his classroom.

Well, it is inevitable. It may be now as later; I have no intention of bowing to his whims.

"You know who I am." This was not a question, but a statement of fact.

"Yes, I know who you are. Do you know who I am?" Justin said.

"Of course, I do," the cleric replied and added, "you no doubt know; what I say goes in this village."

"Does it? Well, what I teach in this classroom is the curriculum set by the Education Department, and it goes without your interference," Justin stated.

A clash of wills, they were now like two swordsmen fighting a dual; thrust and parry.

"I will have to call the principal to sort this out."

"I wouldn't be too rash if I were you; I know all about you," Justin said, then thought,

I do not, but I have you worried, big boy. You are not sure if I know all, whatever that is, or not. Go on, chance your hand; you do not have the guts. I've got you.

The Reverend frowned in his thoughts.

Does he know anything, or is he bluffing? I could call the council, call his bluff, and have him thrown out for threatening a member of the clergy. But what if he knows and tells? Life could become very difficult.

No, I cannot chance it. Negotiate, yes, negotiate.

"Well, we have a difference of opinion here; I will stay out of your class and teachings if you don't interfere in my town."

The Reverend offered his hand; Justin refused it and turned his back.

"Do so," he said.

I have made an enemy for life; I was going to be that before the phony hand offering, anyway. Well, my man, off to a flying start on your first day, and you haven't even met a pupil.

The pupils soon loved Justin, every man jack of them. He greeted his first senior class with a cane in his hand and a stern look on his face. The cane was in common usage, and teachers who used it were not popular with the children. Glum faces stared at him for direction; the image he projected fitted their perception of a teacher chosen by the Reverend.

"That is my name," he said as he pointed to the chalkboard. "So that we stay with school protocol, you will all call me 'Mr. Abbott' or 'sir.'"

"Oh, this is my walking stick. It is not very good. It's too bendy, he showed, and the cane bent over, so he snapped it and threw it in the bin. Now I want you all to come up one by one, starting with this row. Say 'Good morning, Sir,' give your name, then sit down."

This was a method of introduction that he used to gauge the level of discipline within a class. Were they orderly, a rabble, or something between? However, he would handle them, all he needed was the knowledge. He found it difficult to accept what greeted him; they all reacted the same; browbeaten and cowered.

You Luddite Godley! You have stolen youth from these children. Well, I tell you what I intend to restore it.

Justin asked the students, "Write an essay on your thoughts on Wotan and your life in it, plus a second essay on what you wish your life to be when you turn thirty. Have it back in before the end of the month, three weeks away. Although you are writing these as homework, they are for your eyes only. If you wish to share with your family, friends, or the class, that is up to you," he said.

They were all keen on their assignments. They made them think about today and tomorrow. He needed this; he was going to convince these young people that tomorrow belongs to them. How will they use it?

"Any information you share will stay in this room. I give you that guarantee," he said.

This gave the class some comfort. They believed he would respect them and felt confident he was a man of his word. From that point, they were more relaxed in class and responsive to his teaching methods. These methods were New Wave and involved full integration between teacher and class. He was sharing, not giving information, and they were eating out of his hands.

During history in the second week, he asked his class to write half a page on their knowledge of humans' beginning on this earth and hand it in on the next history class. The result was as expected: everyone was a creationist except one effervescent girl, Claire, of the flaming red hair, who was a real eye-catcher. She had that rebellious teenage streak that is common outside of this town. She thought the Reverend was so smart, she would agree with anyone who contradicted his views.

"I have read humans descended from monkeys many years ago."

Claire, one red-haired spark among the dying embers.

He would start the class at a slow pace and expand on the subject.

"I see from your writings that your belief is that God created everything in seven days. If we look back in recorded history, which means written records, we go back to the Mesopotamians, some five thousand years ago. Is this when God created humans? Can anyone answer when? What about a thousand years ago, a million years ago? he asked.

From here, the class became a little confused.

"Have you heard of Homo sapiens from two hundred thousand years ago? Sapiens are the surviving species of the broad name Homo. The ancestors of Homo sapiens were not bred from strict breeding lines like males and females are today. They evolved in various places through the mating of manlike beings. Let me say humans means man and woman; otherwise, we wouldn't be here.

"Have you heard of Neanderthals? They were close relatives who no longer exist. Homo sapiens, us, were the last of the line, and we have inherited the world.

"Scientific history says they were like modern humans. They looked like us, and we descended from them, every one of us. They had our intelligence but not our knowledge or the myriad of tools and equipment that we have at our disposal.

"Imagine—men, women, and children, some of them your age on the cusp of adulthood, were out there wandering in our world all that time ago. What were they up to? Humans' basic needs include survival, self-preservation, sustenance, shelter, and an urge to procreate. After that? Gossip? Needs? Wants? What about the future? Did they think about that?"

He let this sink in.

"These are not the rantings of an unhinged teacher; there is a scientific consensus from a mountain of writings on the subject worldwide. Here, your closed society has not let it in; it doesn't suit their religious teachings. On my desk is a selection of readings on the subject; those that wish may borrow one."

They all rushed out to gather a book. Their titles varied; their topic was all the same: ancient man.

"Take these with you and discuss; you can be sure of one thing: it is the truth."

June, his ex-wife, always said Justin was an expert in creating furors. This time, he excelled. The Village/ Church/ School Council summoned him to an urgent meeting in the kirk. They were before him in all their regalia of office, wearing their three hats. They sat at a trellis table before the altar. A chair facing them at the bottom of the altar steps was for Justin. The townspeople packed the pews behind him; in living memory, this was the town's premier event.

The Reverend was conspicuous by his absence; Justin was certain Godley had made the bullets aimed at his heart. Oliver McGinty chaired the meeting and asked the first question.

"Mr. Abbott, we have summoned you before this tribunal today to answer the charge of gross blasphemy of the Lord. What say you?"

"Under what authority does this self-styled tribunal operate, Mr. McGinty?"

"Under the authority of the New Calvin Kirks of Scotland."

"If that is so, why isn't a representative of the New Calvin Kirks of Scotland present?"

"He is away," was the answer.

"Well, I am of the opinion we adjourn this tribunal until he is back."

Justin turned to face the village people.

"I put it to you, people of this village. Should we adjourn this meeting until Reverend Godley can be in attendance?" Justin asked.

There was a muffled "yes" from the village people.

"There we are, democracy in action. Will you adjourn the meeting, Mr. McGinty? Or will I?"

There was confusion within the tribunal. They were "yes" men incapable of leading. Instead, they followed Justin's suggestion and adjourned the meeting.

A few more knives for my back.

The committee's meek acceptance of his statements surprised him; he had a briefcase full of documentation that confirmed he was teaching the approved subjects; he did not need them.

All cowering lackeys of the Reverend.

At his next history class, a room of eager faces greeted him. They wanted to hear him, see his evidence, and believe him. They were center stage in a contest of wills between the council and their teacher, all cheering for their teacher. Justin was aware of the game and pleased that he had incited a teenage rebellion against the status quo. A silent rebellion, but a rebellion, even so. They hung on his every word, and he supplied a multitude of them.

"Today we will look at our ancient ancestors, a group of twenty or thirty, five, six, or seven families. The family is the basis of all human groups; irrespective of which nation or its government, the family comes first. Some have tried to alter this, such as the communists, resulting in a spectacular failure."

He paused for thought.

"These groups depended on one another for survival. What ethos would govern tribe behavior? Think about it and give me some answers."

All was silent, either not understanding Justin's thrust or not sure enough to offer an answer.

"They relied on rock hard tribal law that protects them. The alternative is internal battles and the disintegration of the tribe," Justin said.

"This system worked until the rise of powerful men, plunders, and thieves; dressed up as noblemen associated with some self-styled leader with a fancy title, lord, count, prince. They were little different from today's Italian Mafia. Even though these people had control, the underlings, most of the communities, existed on their old tribal ethos. This ethos disappeared with newer forms of government. It was the public service's birth; these are people like you and me that governments appoint to manage our affairs. Their mandate grew under successive governments so that they directed all aspects of society. They usurped neighborhoods and clans. Take your problems to the government, and they will fix them. "Do not bother me" became the standard answer; "help thy neighbor" has become redundant: With the government takeover of our lives, we lost our roots in the ancient past, and the crossbreeding of races has confused the issue even more.

"Wotan is a place where I can find continuity out of the cradle of humans. The privilege of having pure links back to the origin of humans is yours."

Justin took a big pause for his big statements. Because of his teachings, Justin now found himself ostracized by the community leaders. They refused to speak to or even acknowledge him, and the Reverend was conspicuous by his absence in school affairs.

I am here for the rest of the year, and I will teach the Education Department curriculum.

He assumed the smug air of the righteous as he battled on.

His pupils were keen on his classes, and he enjoyed teaching them; but the social difficulties of living in the village and their ostracizing him were very trying. At the end of the term, he took leave and spent a few weeks with friends in Edinburgh. He needed a reprieve. He had two weeks until term end and would complete his overview narrative for the students; next term, he would expand his views and cover the finer details.

It was a Monday, and he always spent some time on how the students spent the weekend and their interactions with other people. Here he found solace. The students' feedback told him their parents were keen to hear about the classes. His lessons were becoming subjects of serious discussions within families, and they wanted more.

Ha! I am white-anting the establishment; the Reverend would be beside himself with fury.

In class, he expanded on his narrative of the state's power.

"Directing these bureaucracies are politicians, either elected or part of a ruling clique.

"Have you heard the saying it was a political decision? It is a hindsight statement signifying and excusing an incorrect conclusion. Do not think the rulers decide on what is best for the community? They march to the sound of a different drum. Their reasons are always more complicated than that; they make laws to suit certain pressure groups, appease an ally, enable someone to make money, or make irresponsible policy decisions to manipulate election outcomes."

He paused for comment and answered any queries before he continued.

"Our rulers live in ivory towers and make rules for us citizens that suit them, not us. For example, they decree the state should kill a murderer with no thought to the people affected by such a decision. A death sentence punishes more than the affected; they don't consider this."

A pause for a sink in time, and then he continued.

"What is responsible for the vast majority of violent deaths in our society?" he asked.

'War!" was the universal answer.

"Who decided to go to war?" he asked.

"The government" was the majority decision.

"Governments make laws for society to follow, but they do not follow them," he said, then continued,

"I suggest we move back to our hunter-gatherers. If they had to decide to go to war, who would decide? It would be a consensus decision among the men of the tribe because they would go in harm's way, and the leader would be at the front of the warriors.

You can be sure they made the correct decision. Today we have faceless bureaucrats and politicians deciding. Sitting in their ivory towers with no awareness of the landscape and happenings of the men whose lives are expendable. The wars that have occurred in the past fifty years are responsible for the death of millions of people."

His pacifist views had a philosophical effect on the young students in their sheltered world. Justin transfixed Claire and overwhelmed her with his opinions; she thought he was a special man. Teen-age fantasies of having a deep relationship with Justin were her obsession.

Justin was a consummate storyteller and made history live; he built a picture of the world and its personalities; his narrative combined its environment and power circles. Being in the middle of the developing narrative, the students lived the time and had a deep understanding of the history discussed at the end of their journey. Justin was good at his job; even those within the village who were his enemies had to agree.

At every opportunity, Claire would seek Justin and discuss his subjects. Because she was such a keen student, he gave her his time, but he was always aware of her attraction to him. This was a common occurrence and part of teaching. He was an expert in handling love-struck teenagers and could sidetrack them without offending their sensitivities.

At the end of the third term, all classes take standard Education Department exams. These exams give the teachers an accurate assessment of their students' progress. They are also there to assess the quality of the content presented by the teacher. Before this school break, the School Council summoned Justin to answer questions about the subjects he presented. They did not give him any information, and he did not have an inkling of the reason for the meeting. He countenanced objecting to the department about the meeting, but put this aside; he was confident that he could handle the council as before.

This time it was different; an Education Department bureaucrat chaired the School Council. As soon as Justin appeared, he knew he was at a disadvantage.
The hands of Reverend Godly are all over this meeting.

They were in the school hall; the council and the adviser sat at a trellis table, and Justin sat at a chair before them.

"Mr. Elliot, my name is McInnis, and I represent the Education Department in this matter. Are you aware of the department's criteria and syllabus for teaching history to senior students?"

"Yes," Justin answered.

"May I read you an extract from 'Outcomes' in 'Department Exams'" McInnis said. "Outcome Seven, Section Two. Fifteen percent of marks in any history exam are for stating the exact dates of all happenings as given in the student texts. Your students' results all had excellent marks in subject matter, equal to any school marks under our jurisprudence. However, all scored low on these dates; by your actions, it penalized these students ten marks out of a hundred; one nearly failed because of this."

"Mr. McInnis, sitting next to you are the men of the School Council. Would you hazard a guess at their ages, not their birth dates?" Justin replied.

"I will not take part in these games; of course, I do not know their ages, let alone their birth dates. The gist of all this is that the department states in their outcomes the exact date. You agreed in writing that you would teach the department's curriculum. On any measure, you have ignored their directives and emphasized your criteria. I agree with what you say, but it is not our position to do as we please, or it would render the whole syllabus useless. Anarchy would prevail. Do you have any more to say?"

"No," Justin replied.

"Well, you may leave us."

They dismissed Justin from the school.

On returning from the break, the class was ashen. Group depression, followed by curiosity and anger, were the prevailing emotions of the class. Claire was most upset; after all, she was in love with him and thought she would die. To add fuel to the fire, the replacement was an acolyte of Reverend Godly, another God botherer; the entire community was again under the Reverend's strict control. He would ensure that no more troublemaking interlopers entered their doors.

It takes a powerful intellectual force to quash the blossoming of inquiring youth. The New Kirks of Scotland had achieved this end, and they owned Wotan and every soul that lived in it. Like all her contemporaries, Claire lost her enthusiasm and became another introverted young woman. She finished her schooling that year and did not leave Wotan for the next level of education. Her parents, Osgar and Rhona, were old, and her sister was ten years older than Claire, who was the baby. Big sister had no intention of letting her parents interfere with her brilliant career. She told Claire it was her problem, and to deal with it. Her father had been a successful business manager, but now had advanced rheumatism and was just ambulant. Her mother was a short, rotund woman whose excessive weight played havoc with her legs. Claire loved her parents; they had been good to their little girl all her life; she would not see them abandoned, hence her entrapment in Wotan.

Claire led the life of caregiver and servant of God for the following years, until Callach entered her life. The church from Glasgow had sent him to assist the Reverend at Wotan. He was a firm believer and follower of the Reverend and was an elect who would enter Heaven's gates, on the Reverend's say, of course. Callach was a tall, thin, long-faced man with communication problems; he never smiled.

Chapter 3

It happened at the Easter Ball, their annual dress-up event. Young couples paired at this time of year. It was a tradition in Wotan since the eighteenth century. Now, under Godley's rules, pairing was not for the ball; it was for life. These young people had known one another all their lives. They all knew the personal foibles of their peers. To them, personality made the person, appearance played a minor part. The selection of life's partner was easy. Soul mates drifted together in their teens and stayed for life.

Wotan's rules did not differ from many tribal practices worldwide, where arranged marriages are common. This tradition did not suit the Reverend; it was not of his making. To bring all marriage activities under his control, he decreed he would nominate a couple at God's command. The interfering Reverend was going to cause considerable consternation and angst by overriding tradition.

The Reverend first called Callach. He had no hesitation in calling a rare Celtic beauty, Claire, to come forward to be betrothed to Callach. Claire was on the verge of collapse.
"Why him? Why me? God, please help me," was her silent plea.
Everyone knew that a life of misery awaited her. She went forward as expected, and Godley confirmed their betrothed status. She needed help and went to her mother.
"You have drawn a very short straw, young lady. You must be optimistic. Callach is a product of that miserable church. Your job is to turn him around. If he has one ounce of manhood, he will want you. Lead him on, use

your natural feminine wiles, work at it, don't be despondent."

"You are right, Mum; I must stay optimistic. I will do as you suggest."

She tried; it was heavy weather as Callach was a closed book who would answer everything with yes or no. He did not have any physical contact with Claire; he recoiled from it. His one saving grace, he wasn't at this stage an angry man but a loner lacking in people skills. Claire saw him as little as possible and developed the habit of not expecting any answers and did not ask questions; when they were together, she gave directions. This relationship continued for more than a year. She never asked about marriage. She hoped everyone would forget their betrothal, but the Reverend did not forget. He summoned Callach.

"Callach, since your uncle died, you are now the owner and resident of that extensive property; it needs a family. Your marriage must be at Easter, as you will have waited twelve months. It was ample time to remove any thought of an out-of-wedlock dalliance. This community does not need any of those sinful practices; over the years, some have occurred. I should have known that you would stay pure. I will write about the occasion of the betrothal in the Kirk diary."

Callach did not tell Claire; her mother told her when she saw it in the Kirk diary. It was a small ceremony because Callach did not have family or friends; he was on his own. Claire could have her parents, which suited Claire.

"You wouldn't want your friends attending if you were going to prison. Why here?"

The ceremony comprised the Reverend standing outside the kirk's altar rails and saying,

"Do you, Callach, take this woman to be your wife?"

"Yes," Callach said.

"I now pronounce you man and wife before the witness of God."

That was it. The Reverend turned and disappeared behind the altar rail, and Callach turned and headed out the door. They left Claire and her parents standing. It was too much for Claire; her mother expected her reaction and drew her into her bosom. Claire burst out, crying,

"I have never been more humiliated in all my life than now before those despicable men," she said.

Her angry father said, "If I had my old gun going, I would kill that bastard."

"And I would cheer you on," her mother added.

The three of them went home.

"If Callach wants his wife, he will have to come and get her," Claire's mother said.

Callach's house was the last house at the end of town; it was on its own in the depression. Callach's sole purpose was to grow vegetables and plants for the community. Callach's uncle had been a wealthy man and had built the largest house in town; it was a double- story house and faced into town. Its outlook at the back was onto an area of rolling landscape with gorse and small tree cover. It was the most desirable home in the community. That was on the outside. Inside was another story. It was dark and somber, all the woodwork was dark, the floor coverings were dark, and the little light that reflected was from the discolored ceilings.

Callach was in the settlement when the Reverend accosted him.

"I haven't seen your new wife, Callach. Is she sick?"

"No, Reverend, she hasn't moved in."

Without a word, the Reverend turned and walked to Claire's house, where he banged on the door.

"Claire!" he called.

Claire's mother opened the door.

"Not you; I want Claire. Now!"

A shocked Claire came to the door.

"Go home with Callach now. Do you hear me?" Godley said.

He stood waiting; Claire's father came to the door.

"Who gave you permission to yell at my family?" He was angry.

"I will not countenance any nonsense from you, or I will make your life so miserable you would wish you were dead."

"Leave it, Dad. I will go," Claire said.

She left with Callach to return to his house. The Reverend went to the kirk.

The hide of these people, thinking they can make their own decisions. I will give an appropriate sermon on Sunday.

Claire went to Hades; she was only seventeen. Once she was in the dark and somber house that had not seen a woman's touch in years, she realized how hopeless her plight was.

Callach's first words to Claire were, "I am going to work, clean up here, and prepare my meal." With that, Callach went to his gardens.

It was midafternoon. Even in daylight, Claire struggled to find the light switches. Two downstairs lights were working, one in the kitchen, which doubled as the dining room, and one at the foot of the stairs. She went upstairs. The place was unkempt, unused, and had a seedy, musty smell. The upstairs was composed of bedrooms and one large lounge room; she went downstairs and located Callach's bedroom. It was untidy and had an odor, the smell of an unclean man. She spent the next hour cleaning up the kitchen, the appliances, and the larder. There was some stewing meat in the refrigerator freezer, and she left it out to thaw; she also found enough vegetables in the larder to make a wholesome stew.

Claire's work surprised Callach when he came in. He did not comment, ate, and then returned to his gardens.

So far, so good, Claire thought.

She continued sorting and cleaning, and she had some order by late afternoon. There was scant food in the house; she found a packet of flour and baked fresh bread. The evening meal was fresh bread, butter, and jam, washed down with a pot of tea and some fruit.

"This is all there is available; I would like to head down to Kinlochbervie in the morning and restock the larder. Is this agreeable to you?" Claire asked Callach.

"Write your list and do so. I have an account at McAlfie's store; go there and shop."

"Okay. I will look after myself in the morning," Claire answered.

Claire was up very early and headed down to the wharf to catch the 6:00 a.m. trip on *Esmeralda* to Kinlochbervie. She enjoyed the boat ride away from the prying eyes of Callach, and the chat with the crew on the way down pleased her. Claire had the whole of the day from nine in the morning until five in the evening, when *Esmeralda* returned. She wandered through every shop in town and familiarized herself with them all. As an avid reader and wordsmith with a penchant for the written and spoken word, she spent a long time at the bookshop. At midday, she sat in a little cafe and had tea and sandwiches. She would go to McAlfie's in the afternoon before *Esmeralda* departs. While at the cafe, she picked up the *Edinburgh Chronicle*. Her teenage heart throb was staring from the front page. It missed a beat. He had returned from London, where he was promoting his book *Man's Long Journey*, and would give an early afternoon talk at the town hall two weeks from that day.

I must be here, she told herself.

Claire spent the afternoon planning and was very careful about what she had bought. She must only buy enough essentials for two weeks. She would not miss that presentation.

The crew noticed a change in her demeanor on the way back.

"What's got into you?" one asked.

"I met some friends and lunched with them. It was a pleasant day. Why? Does it show?"

"It does. They must be good friends."

"Yes, they are."

I must change that before we reach Kinlochbervie. I will think of His Horribleness, which will change me.

She returned and trundled to the house with her purchases, packed them away, and looked for something simple for dinner. Callach came in from the gardens and never said a word after the meal. He went to his room. Claire cleaned up and did some preliminary preparations for breakfast. She had been up at dawn that morning and had a book to read that night. Little did she know what was in store.

She was preparing for bed when she heard heavy footsteps on the stairs. It was Callach, stark naked, standing with an erect member, with his mouth twisted in a hideous snarl. He threw her onto the bed, tore the lower clothes from his body, rolled her onto her stomach, and penetrated her anus. She screamed in pain as he thrust out his lust. It took seconds; he lay exhausted.

Upon recovery, he started to beat and punch her.

"You are a sinful, evil Jezebel, put on this earth by the devil to tempt humanity. May you rot in Hell."

Then he left the room as quickly as he had come.

Claire lay in her bed, sobbing.

"My first encounter with my husband leaves me bruised, battered, and brutalized; he is an animal, no, animals are predictable, creatures of habit, he is evil and mad. I cannot live like this. I must see Justin and ask him what to do."

She lay thinking of her plight when she heard a rhythmic outside noise coming from the front of the house. Curiosity overcame the fear of Callach, and she went into the lounge room. Without turning on the light, she could see a figure silhouetted against the night sky. She saw Callach on the cliff edge, naked above the waist and with a flay, whipped his back repeatedly. She watched him for some time, then turned and left the room.

"This man is raving mad, and I am his wife," she shuddered.

The pain in her anus persisted, and there were blood stains on her clothing. She made an appointment to see Dr. Brodie, who was in Wotan on one of his regular visits.

What he saw shocked him.

"How did this happen?"

"Callach forced himself on me."

The doctor was furious.

"This is a dreadful injury. I am going to tell the men of the community. He will be lucky to be alive after they finish."

"Please don't. He is an acolyte of the Reverend, who will create terrible trouble in the community for my parents. I do not want that. Do not worry, I will sort it out."

"I bow to your wishes, irrespective of that I will have to stitch you down there. I will give you a treatment plan for the next few weeks," Dr. Brodie said and added.

"The next time Callach comes to me for treatment, he will receive much more than he expected. I will promise you that."

Irrespectively, life continued until Claire said to Callach as they sat at the breakfast table.

"The larder is getting low, and we need more fresh food and cleaning products; I should go down to Kinlochbervie tomorrow and buy the stock. Is that is all right with you?"

She was nervous and hoped it did not show.

I must see Justin; if I don't, I will not find him again.

"All right, I need some supplies for the garden and will write them down this evening." Callach answered.

"I will be up early in the morning and away. I will not disturb you," Claire said.

Elation flooded her mind. She was lucky. Callach was up from the table and was out the backdoor as she spoke. He had said all he wanted.

She was up in the morning. With Callach's list, she walked down to the berthed *Esmeralda*. An enormous sea was running.

"You will go?" she inquired of the man at the dock.

"Of course. *Esmerelda* won't even notice these few ripples."

She sat indoors near the motor.

"Sit in the center of the boat when the seas are up," a crew member told her. "There's not as much movement from the sea swell." Joy and hope were in her heart as she sat through the rocky journey.

"He will remember me, but will he speak to me?" Doubt was in her mind, and apprehension grew within.

Of course he will.

The boat was late because of the seas and deposited its few passengers. Claire could see that it would be a busy day for the crew, since they had a full load of live sheep as cargo. They would have to remove their droppings and stench before the return journey.

She picked up the supplies from McAlfie's first, then had tea as she read the local paper. Justin was in the paper again. They were expecting a packed house in the town hall. The locals were aware of his work at Wotan, their closest neighboring town.

"I must be first so that I will have a center seat in the front row; then he will notice me."

Claire's front seat was waiting for her. She wasn't first. There was a sprinkling throughout the hall of older residents. The front row was empty. This pleased her. The crowd filtered in, and the hall filled. The senior students from the local high school created a constant hum in the back rows. Then a gentleman walked onto the stage and gave Justin and his work a thorough introduction. Justin came to warm applause and raised his hands to acknowledge the crowd. He noticed Claire and gave her a welcoming smile.

"He has remembered me." A smile lit her face.

Justin spoke to entertain, used overheads, and slides to emphasize his subject, and referred to his books on sale at the backdoor. Here was a celebrity. Claire knew him, and he knew her. She felt so proud. It seemed no time at all, but it was more than an hour and a half before he finished. The crowd flocked around as he signed books for those who had purchased a copy. Claire stood at the back of the crowd and waited for her moment. He glanced at her.

Young Claire, the Celtic beauty, looks very troubled; she wants my time, and she will have it.

When the crowd thinned, he addressed Claire.

"Well, young lady, let us partake of sustenance," he said as he invited her arm through his. "I haven't eaten yet. I like to wait till after my presentations. It is not a good look to have spilled food on your jacket when you speak, and you know what I can be like."

He laughed. He knew she still loved him, not now a teenage crush but something genuine that she felt inside.

"We will duck over to that tavern, and I will have an ale. Do you drink? No, of course not. Still, you may choose something that pleases."

They went to the little tavern. There was a smattering of locals present, but ample vacant booths for them to be comfortable. This was the first time he had experienced it. When Claire walked into the room, it fell silent. Her sophisticated alabaster features and green eyes framed by her long, scarlet hair captivated all. Claire was unaware of her projected aura as she slid into a booth. The room settled.

Justin slid in beside her and spoke.

"I am here. You have troubles. Tell me?"

Claire could not help herself. She burst into tears. Justin did not comfort her. He let her tears run out. She stopped.

"Tell me what happened, précis please, from when you left school."

She gave him an outline of who turned up at the school to replace him. And about the Reverend's iron fist coming down on all, why she could not leave the village, and her forced marriage to Callach. She told him of her brutal raping by Callach and the pain and humiliation she experienced.

"I don't think he is sane, as I saw him in the moonlight after he raped me. His back was bare, and he had a whip. He was whipping his own back. He is mad, isn't he?"

"No, he is not. That is an old religious ritual practiced as an atonement for sins. It's called flagellation." A pause, and then he said,

"The world would be better if someone were to remove that Godley. But that will not happen. What about leaving the village and your so-called husband? That sham marriage is not legal."

"I can't leave. There's Mum and Dad and they are old and need my help. They have lived there all their lives, their friends are there, and they are happy in their little cottage. If they left for me, they would have nothing. No, I could never do that."

"I remember now. No, stay. What we will do is sort out that sick husband. Callach, I remember him, a pathetic product of the New Kirks of Scotland; he is the principal source of your misery. Well, young lady, you are going to be a hard bitch. You will make him terrified of you, so he will be the subservient one.

"Next time he rapes you, that act is the antithesis of making love. It makes me sick.
The next morning, have the biggest and sharpest knife in the kitchen. Stand behind him so that he is not aware of you. Place an armlock around his forehead and push the knife blade hard against his throat. It will give him a slight cut, then say,

'If you come near me again, you die that night. Your blood will cover this house. I will scream as you go to Hell, everyone will come, and I will say I saw an intruder, the police from Glasgow will be here, and your body will be on the front page; you will be famous."

"Then squeeze his head tighter, dig the knife deeper, and say in a loud, guttural voice, "Understand?"

"You will get a meek 'yes,' then punch the side of his head as hard as you can. Practice this and your words. You will scare the living daylights out of him.

Now, the hard part, you must keep a tough exterior. How does that sound?"

"Fantastic! Will you do it for me?"

He laughed.

"You must do it; you know that. Once he rapes you again, you will do it, you will want to do it."

She felt on top of the world.

"Are you married?" she asked.

"No, I am not."

"Will you marry me? I am still in love with you."

You are already married, and I am too old for you. I couldn't cope with your youth and virility."

"Well, will you make love to me?" she asked.

He laughed. "You are incorrigible. No, I will not. Come, I will walk you to the boat and I will give you my contacts if things go wrong. If you feel in danger, call me, and I will be there."

They stood at the dockside next to *Esmeralda*. He looked into her childlike, pleading eyes, which were framed by her red hair.

"Will you kiss me?"

He put his arms around her.

"Close your eyes," he said.

He gave her a full-on kiss as he hugged her to him.

"Now go home and do what you have to do."

She gave him a beautiful smile. "We are friends?"

"We are friends," he replied as he led her to the gangway.

His mind was whirring.

"That was not the kiss of a girl, but that of a sensual young woman, an intelligent young woman." He hated his excitement.

"Get your mind out of there, you old fool," he admonished himself. "That tumultuous world is full of danger."

With that, Claire left Kinlochbervie and headed back to Wotan. Her heart was light, and Justin flooded her mind as the journey proceeded. As she moved into the second hour of the journey, Justin faded from her mind and images of Callach appeared. The lightness of her heart became heavy. She shuddered at what lay ahead.

I would rather die than wait for that monster to strike. I don't need raping to get the courage to act. I will do what I need tomorrow morning and enjoy it, she thought.

Claire came in with her purchases, saw Callach in the garden, waved the garden products she had purchased for him, and left them on a stand at the backdoor. Going into the kitchen, she unpacked the purchases and prepared a light meal for the evening. All this time, her thoughts were on how, not on diversions such as "it's wrong to kill" or "have compassion for your fellow man." She was following her primitive instincts; survive, do whatever you have to achieve your aim.

After the meal, while she was clearing away, she found her retribution weapon. A small length of electrical wire. She concealed this in her jacket and took it to her room, where she tied each end around wooden clothes pegs. She had made herself a garotte.

The next morning, she was up to prepare Callach's breakfast. All was normal. Then her moment came, and without the slightest hesitation, she looped the cord over his head and around his neck. Then pulled the handles on the cord and placed her knees against the back of his chair. She then flopped back so that her body weight was on the wire. She had garroted Callach; all he could do was tear at the wire as it tightened. Anger and hate were high within her as she spoke with considerable venom,

"You are about to spend forever in eternal flames, you monster. Do not pray. God won't listen to you."

His feet were floundering on the floor, as his eyes bulged. Claire kept pulling. His death was imminent. Then she relaxed her weight. The choking stopped, and she heard him gasp some air as she spoke.

"You live today because of my benevolence. If you touch me or come into my bedroom again, you die. This I promise you. Nod your head in acceptance."

He forced out a nod, and she relaxed and removed the garotte. He collapsed onto the floor and wept. She left him and went to her room.

From that moment, he stayed away from her as much as possible and never went up the stairs. Life became livable and continued that way for many months. Although something had changed with Claire, libido was the catalyst. She had joined the library in Kinlochbervie and fell in love with romantic novels. They all progressed to where imagination came to the fore, and a foment of feelings welled within her that flowed through her whole body, culminating in her groin. With these, her whole body would tense; she would moan and stiffen her body as her feelings demanded. The natural extension from this state was exploration, then satisfaction.

* * *

Myor, as with his parents, came from a coastal shipwreck. He was a mute and was in his final year of high school. He was older than the others. His parents kept him at school longer than needed. They thought he would have a void in his life if he left, as all in the village considered him unemployable. His treatment from his peers had changed with puberty; he no longer received benevolence and care; he was in the young male world of dog-eat-dog. As much as he wanted to, his father, Hagen, as a non-Wotan, dared not interfere. For Myor to cope with his future life, he must sort his way through this maze. Ignoring the jibes was natural, and his young man's physique kept most of the aggressive at bay.

There was one group of young men, there always is, under the leadership of Caelian, who was the biggest boy in school and a natural bully. He swaggered about with his pack of lackeys one pace behind him. During the school midday break, Myor was eating his food from a container his mother had prepared when Caelian and his pack approached him. Caelian was there to make trouble.

"Aye, look, the dummy is eating his dog food. Why don't you eat it like a dog?" he said as he pushed Myor's face down into the container.

"I will help you up," the bully said as he slammed Myor's head back into the wall.

Myor stood and attempted to brush the food off his clothes.

"Got ourselves dirty, have we?" Caelian said as he picked some waste from the ground and threw it at Myor.

It all happened in a split second. Myor lifted Caelian, inverted him, and drove him headfirst into the ground. Myor had knocked him unconscious and broke his shoulder. This hushed his group. Myor sat and gathered the remnants of his lunch and ate it with the prostrate Caelian at his feet.

They lied; they said they were walking past when Myor went berserk and attacked Caelian, who was defenseless from such a vicious assault. The next day, Caelian's father was at the school demanding blood.

"My boy is in hospital in Kinlochbervie, and I want the thug who assaulted him thrown out of the school. Now!"

Oliver McGinty and the School Council investigated the incident and expelled Myor from the school. It was not a unanimous resolution; two council members knew the players involved and would not accept the official explanation. Still, Myor was out.

Hagen wasn't disappointed. He knew his son had had his full of schooling, and it was time to move on, so Myor worked at any job Hagen could get for him.

At Callach's farm, life went on in its mundane way until the accident. Heavy rain had saturated the gardens at the farm. With difficulty, Callach loaded his dray with produce. Then he transported his vegetables to the wharf, where they would take it on *Esmeralda* to send to the markets at Kinlochbervie. As his horses attempted to drag the dray through the mud, it became stuck. Callach hopped down from the dray to add his shoulder to the attempt. The dray was inching forward when the rear wheel next to Callach fell into a soft spot. The wheel disappeared up to the axle, and the load on the dray shifted, then toppled; and fell on top of the struggling Callach. His bellow attracted the whole town. Claire was first at the scene. Callach was on his stomach with the weight of the dray on his spine. He was screaming in agony. It was Callach's luck that the doctor was in the village on his weekly visit, and he rushed to the scene. The village men were trying to lift the dray off him and pull his body out.

"Don't touch him or you could break his back!" the doctor yelled.

The doctor worked a flat piece of timber under Callach's prostrate body and gave him a large pain-killer injection. This rendered him semi-conscious, and they carried him down to the wharf, where *Esmeralda* was preparing for the trip to Kinlochbervie. Callach was lucky but still an injured man and would be many months in treatment and rehabilitation. In the blink of an eye, the farm became Claire's responsibility. She tried hard and learned about farming by trial and error and from her neighbors. This worked well, although the heavy work with the horses, dray plow, and spiked harrow was too much for her.

The Reverend Godley injected himself into the equation. One of his anointed ones was in trouble, and he would fix it.

"We must keep the farm viable until Callach returns. Who is working the farm?" he demanded. "Claire, his wife," was not to his liking.

"A woman? This is a man's job," Godley said.

There was not a man in town available to run the farm. Some could assist, but the reluctance to do the job rested on Godley's reputation; nobody would work for him. Then he thought of Myor. "I will see the mute's father and arrange it."

He stormed off to see Hagen, who saw him with open antagonism on his face. Godley's insensitivity blanked the feelings of others, and he was unaware.

"I have arranged a permanent job for your boy. It is at Callach's farm helping while he is in rehabilitation. It will be quite some time before he returns to his farm, and it will be debatable whether he can work it without help. Now, his woman is there on her own and, as with all women, she is not up to the task."

"Will you be taking any part in it?" Hagen suspiciously asked.

"No! I have more important pastoral matters requiring my attention."

"Well, I will take him over to see Claire. He likes her."

When Hagen asked Myor, he thought he saw a glimmer in his eyes. He discussed this with his other, Celena.

"You are reading him. It is about time. He is very excited," his wife said.

Hagen took Myor over to see Claire. As she knew Myor from school, there was no need for an introduction. All she said was, "Hello, Myor." His reply was solid eye contact, a message she received and interpreted. Myor, the man, excited her, and she was sure she excited him.

"When will he start? Will you be paying him?" Hagen asked.

"As soon as possible," Claire said.

"I don't have any money, and even if I did, Callach would stop it when he returns, although Myor can help himself from the garden. If he supplied you with all the food you wanted, you could pay him for it? Would that be acceptable?"

Claire looked at Myor, and they again made eye contact. The silent message of desire passed between them. She knew, and he knew, the electricity that existed between them. An involuntary shudder of desire zapped Claire as she looked away. She knew it was acceptable, and so did Hagen. From this, Myor became an employee.

He appeared the next morning, and Claire was ready for him. He presented in his usual attire, a sleeveless vest and kilt. It was all he wore in summer and winter except in the rain or snow, where he donned an old sheepskin coat. The ignorant in the town said he did not feel cold because of his infirmity. But his muscular build and years of conditioning enabled him to tolerate the conditions.

She knew she could prattle on, and Myor would take in her word. There was no need for eye contact. He was quick on the uptake when he concentrated and soon understood the tasks expected of him; those that need strength. As they worked together, Claire eyed Myor's proud stance and masculine form. It reinforced her conviction that the inevitable must happen. All his beauty did was reinforce her repulsion for Callach's puny, gangling body.

Claire's natural body chemistry was now demanding release from the yearnings within. In her private moments, she was aware of her body and its demands for satisfaction that compelled her to follow. These became an evening ritual where she let her mind build fantasies around her childhood heartthrob Justin. Now these turned to Myor. Claire found these actions gave her temporary relief rather than satisfaction. She had become a prisoner of all-enveloping frustration that gnawed at her; she needed every woman's dream and entitlement.

Bathing, then going to the upstairs lounge, where the sun shone through the picture window, was a rare pleasure for Claire. On these occasions, she robed herself in a light gown that opened at the front, which she let hang open to allow the summer sun to warm her body as she dried her hair. Today the hair hung over her face as she rubbed it with the towel; through the strands of her hair, she saw, down below and watching, the motionless form of Myor. A sexual thrill ran through her as she parted her legs to excite the voyeur without letting on that she was aware of his presence. She felt wonton as she displayed her wares before him. This secret exhibitionism lifted her libido to its highest level; her body screamed with desire. She shrugged off the gown and turned her back as she finished drying her hair.

Claire then turned to face the staring Myor. She made solid eye contact, picked up her clothing, turned, and walked naked out of the room, straight to her bedroom to seek blessed temporary relief for her needs.

It did not go away. It gnawed at her every day, but she remained aloof in her dealings with Myor. Claire realized the folly of any word, with the slightest hint of any impropriety leaking into the community. It would lead to his withdrawal from the farm, and the community's scorn would make life unbearable. This led to continual self-relief and a vicious cycle of frustration.

It had been a hot summer, and on this day, Claire meandered to her secret pond over the hill, and in the bushes behind the house. As the access was through their property, this was her world, and she enjoyed the solitude and freedom it offered. She took her towel, as she often took a dip in the shallow pond in that secluded place. Claire removed her clothes and lay in the bracing shallow water for a few minutes, climbed out, dried herself, and lay on the towel in the warming sunshine.

She spreadeagled herself and let the sunshine fall on her exposed body. As usual, her thoughts turned to sex, and she was aware of her moisture as drowsiness overcame her. She closed her eyes and drifted off into her world of fantasy. Her imagination could feel a rampant penis sliding up and down the moist slit of her vagina, causing her legs to spread wider and upward. She, exposed, thought she felt strong hands slide under her and lift her so the rampant member could penetrate her to the hilt. Claire dared not open her eyes, or her life-changing happening might vanish. She felt hands slip under her shoulders, and she grasped the arms and wrapped her legs around the muscular waist. Claire allowed her body to lift as her head hung back and her eyes stayed shut tightly. The fantasy seducer's powerful arms pulled her shoulders toward him. The penis filled her beyond any fantasy as her head hung from her supported shoulders.

Don't open the eyes, or it might all vanish.

Claire's body was alive with sensation, from her flushed cheeks, reddening neck, and engorged nipples, through her stomach to her blood-flushed vaginal region. She thought she would explode with sensation as he walked farther into the forest. He lowered her; her head touched the grass first, followed by her supported shoulders and then her back. Her legs were still around his waist, and he enveloped her inside and out. Even though she shut her eyes, she felt them roll back as the thrusting started. She moaned with desire, and a grunt of acceptance from deep within emanated with each stroke. With reflex actions, she quickened her movements and grasped his body tighter; she was on a frantic climb to the pinnacle of desire. The higher she went, the quicker the movements. Her mind was not hers; she had surrendered to her wonton feelings.

Then it happened.

She tumbled with convulsive movements from the pinnacle into the clouds of bliss. She no sooner reached this stage than the thrusting recommenced, and she climbed the pinnacle and then, once more, into bliss. No relief once more into the cycle. The sensations had her captured in a climactic pleasure cycle. She was in a place she could not imagine and wanted to stay there forever. How long has it continued? Nobody knew; nobody was measuring. Claire did not know when it culminated. She awoke, the sun was disappearing, and she was lying in the clearing.

What an unbelievable fantasy, she thought.

As she rose to leave, things looked different.

Where are my clothes and my towel? she thought as she looked for an interloper.

"No pond"! She pursued the trail. It was twenty meters until she reached the pond and her clothes. As she dressed, she felt the stickiness. She lifted her finger to her mouth. It was a strong, salty taste.

Man! A real man or a fantasy man? Who or what?

These questions occupied her mind as she returned to the house. Her first thought was Myor. Claire was now adept at reading him, but there was nothing in his demeanor to suggest that this was so. She looked at the men of the tribe in a different light; not the slightest clue came to her. Doubt entered the equation. She did not know what a man's sperm tasted, smelled, or looked like. Her opinion could be wrong. It was a dream.

But what about the new location? she asked herself.

"Sleepwalk!"

She accepted her explanation, sort of. She decided there and then that she must visit to see Justin, as he would have answers.

"Of course, I will see you; come to my private consulting rooms in Edinburgh. I cannot break my schedule to come up there; I will arrange overnight accommodations for you. Next Wednesday would suit me. I have a free afternoon," he said.

Claire interested him; her life and the happenings within were key pieces in his jigsaw of ancient human existence.

"You ring me when you arrive at the bus terminal, and I will pick you up. I am very busy now, so you can give me the complete story on Wednesday. Bye."

Claire informed Myor that she would be away for two days and would notify people in the town. He was to attend to the gardens until she returned.

The trip on *Esmeralda* was without incident. The sea was calm, and they loaded the boat with fish. An enormous flock of squawking seagulls were their constant companions and added color to the trip to Edinburgh. Claire was excited. She loved the thrill and wonder of the big cities. It was one of her ambitions to travel to London and experience the allure of an international city. The knowledge that she was going to see her heartthrob Justin evoked feelings of excitement and sensuality. She was now convinced she loved him.

When the boat arrived at Kinlochbervie, the bus to Edinburgh was waiting. She boarded, and it was on its way. To Claire, it was as though it were waiting for her; she took her seat. The thought of seeing Justin maintained her excitement level. When she arrived at the bus terminal, she rushed to find a telephone and dialed his number. When he answered, there were no formalities. All he received was an excited voice saying,

"I'm here."

He laughed into the phone.

"So, you are. I will drive down and pick you up. Stay at the terminal. I will be there in ten minutes. See you then."

As he approached, he had no trouble spotting her.

"*There she is,*" he thought as the sun highlighted the sheen on the folds of her flaming red hair. Her elegant face lit up, and she was beaming at him as he pulled up.

I have seen nothing so eye-catching as the beauty that has blossomed with her womanhood.

"Well, young Claire, hop in," Justin said as his car glided to a stop beside her.

She slid into the seat beside him and threw herself at him, embracing him as she gave him a big wet kiss on the cheek. He laughed as he said,

"I have never received a greeting like that; I enjoyed it."

He took her hand and said, "Now settle down. We will have a snack and a cup of tea, and then we will go to my rooms for a chat."

"You make me feel very excited, Justin; I still love you; you know."

"Yes, I know."

"Well then, will you make love with me?"

"No, I won't; we are going to eat, and then we are going to my office for you to tell your story."

"All right, later," she finished.

A hand of atrocious cards dealt by life hastened her transition from girl to mature woman. She is still a girl in disposition, a joyous breath of fresh air, without inhibitions or restraint. Life must have been very simple all those years ago.

While they were drinking tea, she talked about all the happenings at Wotan and her life with the warped-minded Callach. Justin's nemesis, the Reverend Godly, was still in control of Wotan. She wanted to blurt out the details of her painful sexual experience. He stopped that.

The natural way she walked through Edinburgh caused everybody to stop and stare, but she was unaware of it. This never happened in Wotan, as she had been part of them all her life. Her peers and the general community knew her foibles and character traits, the actual impressions of a person, not instant impressions.

"You have attracted the attention of half the patrons in here already; wait till you arrive at the office," he admonished her.

Claire quieted and remained calm while driving to Justin's office. It was in a smaller ornate building, and his office suite was akin to a traditional solicitor's room, albeit an untidy solicitor. It impressed Claire. They sat in a small client waiting room, where Justin said,

"Now tell me your story."

Claire told her story in graphic detail. Justin did not interrupt. He listened until she finished.

"Well, that's a very interesting story. Do you think what happened was a figment of your fertile imagination? Think before you answer, it is important."

Claire was silent as she thought.

"Yes, it must be. I had my eyes closed, which says daydream and I was asleep."

"How do you explain the two locations?" Justin asked.

"Sleepwalk."

"Have you ever sleepwalked?"

"No. You don't believe me, do you, Justin?"

"It's not a matter of not believing you. If sleepwalking was not the case, it would complicate your life, so you would rather the happening was in your mind. Do you think that could be?"

Claire thought long and hard. "Yes," was her answer.

"Would you like to know what I think?"

"Tell me."

"You have had a sexual experience that most women would die for. With your eyes shut and not a word spoken, you did not know your partner, and you were alone in your sexual experience. You know that should be impossible? But you can contact your primitive self. The cave woman within compelled you to act as you did.

"Modern woman cannot achieve this without considering her partner's demands and wants. What will their partner think of them after the fire has gone out? Did he enjoy it? Did she please him? Isn't modern life complicated? You are outside all that; your compulsion was to yourself; lucky woman, very lucky woman. Well, what do you think of that hypothesis?"

"Those are your thoughts," she said.

"Let's look at the evidence; you had been asleep and were in a mental state that made you ripe for an encounter. Your mind was on this very subject when it all happened. Whoever consumed you was very strong to impale you on his penis and lift you. What power in those thighs, what power in those arms to lift you? This was not your average man. No sound came from his mouth," Justin said.

"I know who you think it was, Myor. That is who I first suspected. I know Myor, I can read him, and I know what is on his mind. We converse all the time during his work, not speaking but with unspoken words. I returned to the house and accused him; I knew I would get a reaction if it was true; he would avert my gaze, look away or walk off. None of these happened; he gazed at me with a blank stare as though he did not know what I was speaking about. No, it wasn't Myor. I walked around the village and gave any male of stout physique a knowing smile. The reaction I received was a "What's wrong with you?" look. This has me puzzled and led to the fantasy answer," Claire said.

"Well, what about the sperm? Your explanation was an apt description that said, real. There is but one answer; you know Myor. What else would have let him think you have an interest in him?"

Claire thought long and hard before she answered.

"I exposed myself to him."

"Oh? How did this happen?"

"I had finished bathing and was standing in a flimsy gown in front of the picture window that overlooks the back garden. I was drying my hair when I spied him looking up at me. I pretended I had not seen him and put on quite a show. I became aroused, stripped, and displayed my body to him; it was very erotic," Claire said.

"For both of you. Myor is our man. You have had an experience and reached the heights that ordinary woman can only dream of. Lucky girl."

"What are you suggesting? I'm different?" An annoyance in her voice.

"Yes, I am. You and some of your contemporaries."

"Is this difference the reason for your interest in me?" A coldness entered her voice.

Justin moved, sat next to her on the sofa, and put his arm around her shoulders.

"I have never lied to you, and I do not intend to start now. That was one reason I came to Wotan, to see if the links to ancient people existed in your tribe. Why was I attracted to you because you were a feisty young woman, not cowered like the others by Godly, but prepared to stand by your independent views? I believed that when they threw me out of school, that would be the end. But no, like a ray of sunshine, you re-entered my life, and I am very glad," Justin said.

He looked down at her bowed face and saw that she was crying. Compassion welled within him.

"What's wrong, little one? Tell me," he said.

She looked at him through her teary eyes.

"I'm scared, Justin, scared of the Wotan seed I carry. It was as easy as breathing. I could have killed Callach when I choked him. He was not of our tribe, and I had no compassion. Nothing within said stop. You are my pillar, someone to tell and give me directions. Don't you let me down, Justin, or I will die."

She turned, and he wrapped his arms around her and whispered in her ear,
"I will never let you down."

The tears came again, but they were different tears, ones of hope. Justin held her to him, and they were quiet. He sat there, as if a lightning bolt had struck him.

You moron, you are a stupid, stuck-up moron. You had not thought of her or what was happening to her. Your interest is your bloody theories."

"Claire, I will be your mentor for life. I want you to contact me every week, at the least, on any matter. I will always be there," he said.

They were quiet again, and he said to himself,

Now is the time to be honest and face life's realities. Yes, I am more than twenty years older than she is; irrespective of anything, I love her; there I got it out: not as a daughter or a friend but as a beautiful young woman whom I want to live with for the rest of my life.

Claire, now roused, stretched her arms above her head.
How desirable is she? he thought.

Justin was about to say something when panic struck.

I am an infatuated old fool. She is a married woman and has problems to sort out. Stop dreaming.

Justin let it hang for the moment.

They were circumspect as they readied to drop Claire at the bus stop. As soon as they stopped, Claire kissed him and thanked him. She looked him in the eyes and spoke.

"Justin, I love you."

"And I love you," he replied.

What he said shocked him, but it was out now, out forever.

"Oh, Justin." That was all she said as her eyes misted. She hugged him and gave him the most sensuous of eyes closed kisses from the heart. He reacted to his feelings and accepted all that she was offering.

"What does this mean for us?" she asked.

"At the moment, we will bask in the knowledge, then later plan our future. Go home for now and keep this secret."

Chapter 4

Claire was happy as she returned to Wotan. As soon as she reached home, everything changed. Callach had returned. He was sitting in a wheelchair in the kitchen.

"You Jezebel! I know that you have been fornicating with that mute. All the village knows. May you burn in the eternal fires and your soul be banished to the deepest corner of Hell."

His tirades were of no consequence to Claire; what worried her was "all the village knows."

Who knows what? It must be by inference. All contact with Myor is here, and nobody knows, or do they? Her mind was whirring.

"Ha got you! I knew you couldn't hide it." Callach said in triumph.

"I don't care what you think, you warped cripple."

The word "cripple" drove him into a frenzy, as Claire knew it would. He had a coughing fit, and Claire, worried about the gossip Callach could spread, left him. Her first thought was to ring Justin, but she did not want to be a nuisance, and she needed immediate action. She sorted it out herself; she returned to the kitchen, pulled up a chair, and sat opposite Callach, eyeball to eyeball.

"Callach, when we first came to this house, you didn't come near me until you ravaged me. I have not told a soul. The village people hate this type of behavior. If I were to walk out that door, approach the village men and tell them about your actions, they would beat you to within an inch of your life or farther. I swear that if you say one word about Myor or me, one word about anything at all, I will inform the men of your behavior. You are unpopular with many here because of your contact with Reverend Godley. Do you hear me?"

The feeble "yes" of a beaten man was his reply.

"Good; I will prepare you a meal. What is your preference?" Claire said, proud of how she handled the incident.

Callach was not a fool and knew he would have to rely on Claire for his existence.

If this back pain would stop.

Life moved on, in a fashion, with Myor and Claire tending to the gardens. Their sexual activities did not stop; they went farther underground. Claire knew that if she could secrete Myor into her bedroom, they would be secure in their lovemaking, as Callach could not climb the stairs. She knew she could do anything they chose, although if Callach knew, it wouldn't be the same. Her mind would equate his presence as being that of a voyeur.

Callach's infirmity prevented him from venturing far from the house, as his wheelchair did not suit the rough terrain. He had no friends in Wotan, and his sole visitor was the doctor on his weekly visit to Wotan. This state existed for many weeks before Callach requested Roy, a young man who worked on *Esmeralda*.

He now had his contact, and a weekly supply of cheap whiskey arrived. Over the weeks, this supply increased until Callach lived his life in alcoholic isolation. Either it was the pain, the alcohol, or a combination that changed his disposition from a broken man dependent on others to a violent confrontational animal. He roamed the house hall in his wheelchair and carried a cane for when he needed to stand. Every time he saw Claire, he would insult her with cries of "Wonton slut," "Jezebel," or any other name that came to mind, then try to hit her with his cane. The insults or the swinging cane did not worry Claire. She would have deaf ears and could evade the swinging cane.

She was in a quandary over her love for Justin and the demands of her active libido that needed Myor. What should she do? She did not dare discuss it with Justin. It is possible that she might hurt him. She decided she would live with the guilt, not realizing that Justin had not demanded she change her lifestyle. Keeping the same as before was the best way. They could not go public about their mutual desire as she was a married woman, and divorce was out of the question in Wotan.

It was late at night when she heard a ruckus downstairs. Throwing on a gown, she crept down the stairs. There was Callach, slurring drunk in his wheelchair, arguing with some imagined enemy. He was shouting and swinging his cane when he saw Claire standing in the hallway before him.

"Jezebel may the wrath of God visit you and stay forever!" he shouted as he struck out at her. Callach then pushed himself out of his wheelchair and stood before her for a moment before collapsing on the floor. He rolled onto his back and continued firing profanities and insults. He had worked himself into a rage; his face turned red, and his eyes were popping. For a moment, he stopped; then, in one colossal heave, the contents of his stomach belched out of his mouth as he was taking a breath. He sucked his bile juices into his lungs as he lay still, gurgling like a baby. Unable to roll, he was drowning in his vomit and looked at Claire for help. She stood and watched him for some minutes until his miserable life left him, then turned and walked up the stairs to bed. She slept well. The next morning when she awoke, she had no emotion.

They called the doctor, who pronounced accidental death because of intoxication. The Reverend came and took the body back to his church.

That is when she phoned Justin. He listened and said,

"Claire, under similar circumstances; half the woman in Wotan would react the same way."

"You say that to make me feel better? Is there something wrong with me, Justin? You said I was different; why and how different?" Claire said.

"I told you I wouldn't lie to you, and I won't," Justin said.

Hearing Justin's voice reminded her of her association with Myor and filled her with guilt. Then Justin said he would come up, but Claire stopped him; she needed time to sort things out.

"It would be better to have a mourning period before I appear. I don't want everyone speaking about us," she said.

"You are right; I won't come until you call me."

With that, they hung up.

The Village Council summoned Claire to a meeting. These bring bad news; Claire approached the meeting with trepidation. She had a tightness in her chest that relaxed when Oliver McGinty stated that the purpose of the meeting was to complete Callach's estate.

"Madam, we are here today to state Wotan rules under which we will complete the estate. As Callach had no other heirs and did not leave his last will and testament, his entire estate here in Wotan becomes your property. As far as we can find out, the house, garden, and all inclusions are free of encumbrances, and they now become your property. He also has a positive bank balance in Kinlochbervie of four thousand eight hundred and twenty pounds. We have included this in the estate.

"Of course, you will leave this to the church."

Claire decided that these church lackeys, people she despised, would not direct her.

"No, I will not; I do not have any funds. Callach was, how will I say, a frugal man, and the estate needs many repairs. I will spend the money on these. There are many items in the house that I will select and donate to the church. Do not badger me. If you give me a copy of all the relevant papers, I will take them to a solicitor in Kinlochbervie and then give you further guidance. With that, she stood and walked out; she couldn't keep the smile off her face.

I will paint the house, give anything that reminds me of Callach to the church. It is all junk anyway, and then renew the furniture.
I must phone Justin, tell him the news, and ask him about a solicitor.

Claire rang Justin to tell him about her good fortune. He laughed.

"Apoplexy must have endangered the Reverend's life when he heard that. He would have already been counting the money as his. Good for you sticking it up them. You need an excellent solicitor. I will find one to suit and get them to ring them."

"Good; that was what I was phoning you about. It is also an excuse to hear your voice. You make me happy."

Claire and Myor's hormone-laden demands, no longer having Callach's presence as a restraint, knew no bounds. These encounters worried Claire: she felt deviate; it must be wrong, but it was so good; if it was deviate, she was a deviate, so be it. They found many ways and places. Their body excitements led to frequent encounters in the house whenever libido called. They lived as though they were the last people on the earth until reality called and reminded them.

Someone started the gossip, and Claire could not stop it once it started. It came back to the lovers, and Claire, panic-struck, suggested that Myor take leave and return to his home for a few weeks. The break gave her time to rationalize her situation and examine her predicament. She knew she had to call Justin. He was the one she wanted. He would be her lover and partner and could restrict her impetuous behavior. She needed him, and she loved him. She decided he would not live with her, knowing of her sinful behavior with Myor. When the word came out, all and sundry would concur that she had corrupted the mute for her carnal pleasures. There was no way she could communicate with Myor to end the association. There was no place for the three of them in Wotan; one must go, and from her reasoning, Myor, not being of the tribe and for her survival, it must be Myor.

How? It had to be a credible accident so that the entire village would accept it. This occupied her mind over the next few days as she devised her survival plan.

On the property was an old, homemade, horse-drawn harrow. It was in a lattice design, four feet wide and six feet long, with six-inch spikes, six to the square foot. It was made to draw over the garden soil to prepare it for planting. The original design was unsuccessful because the front end dug in instead of running through the soil. They bolted two twelve-foot lengths of bearer timber to either side to prevent this. The timber overhang at the rear gave the harrow stability and weight to perform its task. When not used, they pulled it to the vertical by rope and pulley bolted up high on the shed, then secured the loop of the rope around a bolt inserted into the shed wall. They stored it, spikes out, on its timber lengths, against the shed wall.

The bolt holding the rope presented Claire a way when she walked out of the shed and scraped her leg. From here, her planning started. She stood and examined the harrow and saw that the bolt was all that held it vertical. If the rope came off that bolt, the harrow, spikes first, would fall. Its weight and height would guarantee the fall of the harrow. Without the spikes, the harrow would inflict considerable damage to anyone underneath. With the spikes, the impact would be fatal. She had found her way.

A loop with a simple knot hooked the rope over the bolt. If that knot came undone, the harrow would fall. Perfect. Now to position Myor in the death zone. She calculated the height of the harrow and stepped out to the spot where the spikes would fall. She would have to pause Myor and drop the harrow without him being aware. If he noticed it falling, he would evade it. She knew that she would have one chance. The bait was a little red pocket purse she always carried with her. She would place this purse in the death zone, wait till Myor was in the line of sight in the garden, and call him to her. He would walk toward her, see the purse, bend to pick it up, and at that moment she would drop the harrow.

Her impetuosity and tribal mind governed her behavior; she was operating on ancient instincts. Two men and one woman. The ancient Wotan code directed the two would decide the issue. Here, she had chosen the man; she must kill the unchosen to restore the gender balance. Single-minded purpose governed her actions. She had no thoughts on what the future might hold; how the villagers would accept the death; or, most of all, what effect killing her lover would have on her?

As with everything with Claire, it must happen now. She did not have the wise mind of Justin to guide her and thwart her plan. She decided there and then that she would do it tomorrow on the first day of Myor's return.

Myor turned up on time, made eye contact with Claire, and started his first task: weeding the gardens. Claire decided now was the moment. She placed the purse on the spot and waited at her action station at the shed. It was not long before Myor was in the line of sight in the garden.

"Myor, I need you up here now!"

He looked up. "Come, Myor, come, I need you now," Claire repeated.

He stood and walked toward her. There was no anticipation or nervousness in Claire's disposition. He walked toward her. His face, as always, was bland. As he neared the shed, he noticed the red purse. He had seen it often and knew that it was Claire's. He bent to pick it up. Claire released the rope; then reality struck as the harrow moved from the shed wall.

"No. No!" emitted from her mouth as she clutched at the rope and tried to stop the falling harrow. As much as she tried, she could not. The weight was too much as it pulled her hand down and her knuckle smashed into the ring bolt as the rope ran through her hand. Myor looked up and fell onto his back as he tried to catch the plummeting frame. There was no chance, and the spikes hit him on his torso from his neck to his thighs; many spikes had pierced his body. He looked at Claire with anguish. He felt the hurt of betrayal.

As he looked into her eyes, he stuttered the last words of his brief life in a high-pitched, weak voice.

"But I love you. Why?" as his life passed away.

Claire rushed and threw herself on top of him.

It was not a cry; it was a roar from the very portals of Hades; a roar of the damned as Claire screamed her feelings. It ran around the village, so loud and anguished. It seemed to go on for an eternity. Everybody heard it, shocked; they ran to its source. Claire lay on Myor's staring dead body, his anguish in his death mask. She was sobbing over and over.

"Forgive me, Myor, please forgive me. I didn't mean it. It's not what I really wanted."

Chapter 5

"Justin, come quickly. Myor is dead." A quivering and distraught voice echoed over the phone. He recognized it: Rhonda, Claire's mother. He made to question her, but the phone was dead. It was not a conversation; it was an order. He was in a quandary about what to do. How did it happen? Was Claire involved? He decided.

She will need me; I must go there.

It was not yet midday, and the boat did not leave Kinlochbervie until five. He was in his office and spoke to his part-time secretary.

"Mary, cancel all my appointments and engagements, no ifs, no buts. There is trouble at Wotan, and I must go there with haste. I am going home to pack. I will ring you in a few days and let you know what is happening. I will take my personal journal; any business calls you can decide. I know I can trust you."

With that, he was out the office door and home. As he was packing an overnight bag, he stopped and thought.

Get your brain in order before you go flying off. Ring Jim Brodie, the circuit doctor, and the local police to ensure they were coming.

The village had notified Dr. Brodie, the circuit doctor, and he would be on the boat. The local police told him they had heard of an incident at Wotan, and a senior constable would also be on the boat. As there had been a violent death, a detective from Edinburgh would be with him.

It is going to be an interesting trip, Justin thought.

The two police officers were there. He knew Bert Tinkler, a large senior constable, and they introduced him to Detective Sergeant Edgar Fraser.

"Call me Ed," he said. Fraser was of average height, muscular, and looked like a very experienced, no-nonsense type. Ed was straight on the case.

"Justin, what do you know about this?" he asked.

"Not much; the mother of Claire, a young woman I know, rang me, and told me Myor had died. How or when, I do not know, but I assume this morning."

"Who is Myor?" the detective asked.

"He is a mute. A young man born and bred in the community who works in Claire's market garden. She supplies vegetables for the local community and to the people here at Kinlochbervie."

Justin looked at Constable Tinkler.

"You would know her, Bert? The one with flaming red hair."

"I know her, your friend. A rare Celtic beauty." Tinkler replied.

"Friend of yours, aye. It appears everyone knows everybody up there?" The detective said.

"That they do," Bert replied.

The red-faced and flustered doctor turned up as the boat was loading.

"I have delivered a baby, and here I am going to a death. As well as that, I have people all over calling me; there is a virus doing the rounds now. The boat trip and a night off will do me a world of good. Justin, do I know the dead person?"

"You would; he is mute."

"Oh no, Myor. Do you know what happened?"

"No more than you."

The boat was ready, and they boarded. Justin and the detective seated themselves together. The detective, who, as is his calling, had a very inquiring mind.

"What will I find up here?" he asked Justin.

"They built a community unlike any other."
The statement surprised the detective.

"What do you mean?" Ed inquired.

"We have some time, so I will tell you the story; it will be essential that you know it to understand Wotan and its people. Justin took more than half an hour to explain Wotan, its history, and its people. The major point that he made was on its value system.

"Are you telling me they would have no compunction killing me if I were not from their tribe?" Ed asked.

"If you threatened the tribe or one of its members, none. That does not mean there are murders everywhere. Most of the people there are Wotans, anyway. This is the first murder recorded in the settlement. There are no fistfights, either. They are a temperate and peaceful group." Justin answered.

"Are you from Wotan?" Ed asked.

"No, I am not. They sent me there as a schoolteacher, so I know its people and values," Justin said.

"Is this Myor a local?"

"No. He is a survivor of a shipwreck many years ago.

"Is this Claire a local?"

"She is."

"Will the community clam up?" Ed asked.

"No, anything but, everyone will have a theory. Most of them are based on their likes and dislikes. I will warn you that you will encounter a large, opinionated holy man, the Reverend Godley. You will find out his character soon enough. All his followers will enter the gates of Heaven. He dooms all others to the fires of hell. Not reliable witness material," Justin offered.

Ed thanked them for that.

This detective doesn't waste any time.

The boat arrived, and they all went to their prearranged places, except Justin. He headed to Claire's house. Here to greet him were Claire's parents, Osgar and Rhonda.

"Oh, we're so glad you are here. She is in a dreadful state. She is upstairs in the attic room. Please go up to her."

Justin did not need further prompting, he was upstairs posthaste. He pushed open the door to the room. Before him was Claire, back toward him, coiled in a fetal position. He lay on the bed beside her and wrapped his arms around her. She placed her hands on his arms and cried. Justin lay still until she cried out, and then he said,

"You're safe now, Claire. I will look after things."

More tears. He let them run their course as he lay next to her. They stayed in this position for a long time, until Justin's lower arm was getting pins and needles.

"Claire, my body says I must move. You do the same. You cannot spend your life here."

She did not move. Justin extricated himself, straightened her body, and said,

"Come on, we are getting up. You have been in your bed long enough. Life will not pass you by. The doctor and some police officers are here to see you. No, you are not in trouble; there has been a death, and we must make reports."

She rolled over and straightened up.

"I am not sure I can cope with all this," she said.

"First, tell me what happened and about what you were thinking. I knew something would develop after your, will we say, dream? You are a virile young woman entering the complex web of adult personal relationships. I would not think you would react different to all who came before you. This inborn instinct, so important for the continuation of humanity, is in all of us."

It was the first time since he came; she made eye contact.

"I need to know the truth, Claire, to sort this out so we can move forward. Were you lovers?"

"Yes! That is where my sins began."

"Guilt, bah! Nothing can undo the past. I have a perception of what went on; it was a matter of simple deduction. Considering your close contact and mutual attraction, it would take restraint beyond the bounds of humanity. I expected that, and I also expected you to understand. To answer the Myor question, I left it for you. I knew it would be difficult, too difficult; it appears."

She ruminated. She loved Justin and trusted him. He was her main confidant in the world.

"You are right about my association with Myor. It was as you thought. We were at it all the time. We did things I know must be sinful and perverted. It lost me in a sea of depravity. We were addicted to it."

"What you consider depravity is in common usage in many of the households in Wotan, in many of the households in the world. How did you intend to climb out of your quandary?"

"I reasoned there was me, Myor, and you; one had to go. That would have to be Myor, or even me?"

She had used traits from way before, from her tribal instincts. Way back in the days when it was every person for themselves. A woman cannot have two men; they should fight to the death. Might is right; to the victor goes the spoils. She would have to kill one and kill one she did. What a tangled life she has."

"I knew I couldn't tell Myor or his family," she continued. "Imagine the commotion. 'That Jezebel corrupted that poor mute for her carnal pleasures.' They would have forced me out of Wotan. Rumors are already spreading, and his mother 'knows,' and hates me."

"In passing, I noticed the harrow against the wall and started planning. When he walked toward the trap, I realized what I was doing. It was madness, and I tried to stop it. I was not strong enough. I killed him. I killed a man I loved," she said and broke into uncontrollable tears.

"That's enough for now. In the end, you didn't want it to happen. You cannot tell anyone what you have told me, as it raises many other questions. We must develop a story that is truthful. We do not want others to probe, or they will concoct a story that suits their biases, and you could go to jail," Justin explained.

"That is where I deserve to be," she said.

Angry, Justin addressed her.

"Forget that hangdog business. This has been a terrible incident. We will put that behind us and not be part of the bureaucratic condemnation process. I will have the doctor in to examine you. You will say nothing unless he asks, when you will answer,

"'The harrow fell on Myor.' Nothing else. I will be with you when you make a statement to the detective."

He looked at her.

"Look at me. This is all going to happen now. I want you to go to the shower, take a change of clothes, and freshen up. One other thing. I will look after you." He gave her a reassuring hug.

There was a knock on the front door. Justin answered. It was Dr. Brodie.

"I am glad you have come. Claire is getting out of the shower. She is in a dreadful state."

"I imagined that. I have come from examining the boy's body, not a pretty sight. I will give her something to calm her down. May I come in?"

"I am sorry. I should have let you straight in. Come in, come in."

He stepped in as Claire came into the room.

"Ah, here you are, young lady. Not feeling the best, I gather."

"No, I am not." She liked Dr. Brodie; he had been her doctor since her birth. She trusted him.

"Let me examine you. Do you have any pain or strains from the accident?"

Claire sat down, and the doctor sat next to her.

"No, I am all right except for my hand," Claire said. Justin did not know she had injuries.

Dr. Brodie examined the hand.

"Young lady, you have a fractured knuckle on that hand. Where did you get that?"

"When the harrow fell, I tried to stop it by holding the rope. I wasn't strong enough, and it pulled my hand into the holding ring," Claire explained.

"Nasty. Well, you are coming back with me to Kinlochbervie to have an X-ray."

"Tell me, doctor, did you sign the death certificate?" Justin asked.

"No. The detective told me to leave it until he has finished his enquiries. It looks as though we will take the body back on the boat. It will have to go to a coroner's inquiry, and the Crown Office and the Procurator Fiscal Service. You know them?"

Justin did, but for the benefit of Claire, he said, "Tell us."

"The Sherriff's Office handles all hearing actions in Scotland if the cause of death is unclear. Everyone in the village has a theory since Myor's death. The coroner will sort it all out," the doctor said.

Bert Tinkler spent some time at the scene of the accident. He took copious notes, paced out his distances, and took a statement from Claire. A description of the scene and the positions of Myor and herself before, during, and after the event was what he wanted. He took his notes, and that was that. It was easy for Claire.

Detective Ed Fraser was different. He came from a different angle altogether. He showed interest in words from a babble of mouths, some with axes to grind, others with secondhand information. He listened to them all. He knew the answers were in this potpourri.

Detective Ed Fraser visited them at the house. Justin knew why he was there and invited him in. They sat at the kitchen table.

"Tea?" Justin asked.

"No thanks, some answers."

Straight to business.

"Claire, tell me about your relationship with Myor," Ed said.

Claire, scared, looked at Justin, who said. "Claire had known Myor since childhood."

Ed said in a quiet voice loaded with menace, "I don't want to evict you from the room, but I will if you say another word while I am questioning Claire. Understand?"

"I have received the message, loud and clear. Silent I will be," Justin answered.

He who must be obeyed.

"Claire, I have no opinions on any happenings. All I am doing is taking statements. I will take them from everybody here that has something to say. This is all routine in any death scene, whether a motor crash or a murder. I take statements, and the powers to be decide what action to take. If you can help, that will be great. I will ask again. Tell me about your relationship with Myor," Ed said.

"Myor and I were lovers. That is why I am so upset."

"Tell me about him."

"He was mute and noncommunicative with people. They thought he was simple-minded. They are wrong. I have known him all his life, and when he put his mind to it, he was a normal person. Justin knows this," Claire said.

Ed looked at Justin. "I concur. I was his schoolteacher."

"Claire, we will go into the yard, and you could run through the whole happening."
Justin was worried about how Claire would stand up to the questioning of strangers.

I have sold her short again. She had suppressed her feelings of guilt and told it as she saw it. Good for her.

The three of them walked to the back of the shed. The harrow was still on the ground.

"We will re-create the scene as it was at Myor's death. I know this will be difficult for you, Claire, but it must happen," Ed said.

Claire gave him a forlorn look, realizing that she must do it. She knew she would relive her trauma, but was not sure she could do it. Ed took her silence for agreement for the re-creation.

"First thing, Justin and I will place the harrow against the wall."

They stood on either side, lifted the end, and pushed it against the shed.

"It is quite a weight. I have never seen a harrow like this. Why the heavy timbers?"

"The old harrow dug its nose in. The timbers force it to ride flat. They are quite effective." Justin said.

"Yes, I can see that. Good idea," Ed said.

Under Claire's direction, they positioned the harrow as close as possible to where it was on the fateful day. Claire then began attaching the unknotted rope to the tie spike.

"Is that rope always like that? The twisted unblemished section suggests a knot," Ed said.

"The knot was fraying, so I undid it," Claire answered.

"When was that?"

"Before the accident. I was going to ask Myor to retie it," she answered.

Ed thought for a time, then said,

"Justin, could you play the part of Myor? We will walk over to where he was working.

"Stand there, please, Justin," Ed said.

Claire and Ed walked back to where she stood at the time of the accident.

"Now, Claire, I want you to call to Justin as you called to Myor."

Claire called "Myor."

He expected Claire to call Justin.

She will not explain the situation; she is going to relive it. I did not want this.

Justin walked toward them.

I dislike this; she will break down. Justin thought as he walked to the death spot, stopped, looked at Claire, and then looked up at the harrow spikes. It was a chilling sight.

"Walk away, Justin," Ed said and then to Claire. "Let the rope go."

The harrow moved off the wall and then crashed onto the ground. A scream emitted from Claire, and she slumped to the ground, sobbing.

Justin, angry, shouted at Ed, "You callous copper bastard! Did you have to do that?!"

Ed was proud of his control in all situations. Here he lost it. He was not worried about Justin's angry retort; Claire was his concern.

He sat beside her, placed his arm around her shoulders, and tried to console her. Justin, concerned, let it play out. Two men beside her would be too much.

Justin, his anger subsided, said, "That will do for today."

Ed stood, and without a word, walked away. Justin sat beside Claire, placed his arm around her shoulders, and let her cry her remorse out. If Ed had more to ask, he let it be.

In the morning, they headed to the wharf and bordered *Esmeralda*. Justin and Claire sat at the rear of the passenger area. The police were already on board and sat at the front. The doctor sat with Claire and Justin.

"Well, young lady, as soon as we arrive, I want you to have that hand X-rayed. You know where to go, Justin?"

"Yes."

"I have phoned them, and they will be waiting. We will look at the pictures and decide. I can move it into shape with a local anesthetic. It will not be in plaster; I will splint and bandage it. How does that sound, young lady?"

"Fine. Thank you."

When they berthed at Kinlochbervie, the police were first to embark. Ed avoided eye contact as they followed the police down the gangway. Justin and Claire went to the radiology center and then to the doctor. They took a couple of hours to fix everything. Justin did not know what the procedures would be from here. He did not want to approach Ed but had heard there would be a coroner's inquiry at the Procurator Fiscal premises in Stirling, a town on the eastern side of Scotland. He knew Stirling; it was less than an hour's drive from his home in Edinburgh.

"We will take the bus down to Edinburgh, go to my place, pick up my car, and drive up the road to Stirling, where you will see the Coroner's Court. If we are lucky, we can sit in on an inquest and observe," Justin explained to Claire.

"When is Myor's hearing?" she asked.

"We will find out on the court schedule when we are up there."

They arrived at the same bus terminal Claire used on her last journey to Edinburgh.

"We are on the other side of the city center to my abode. We will walk there. Our trip will take us through the city center, where we will stop for a snack. We are half an hour from my home. Stretching the legs is what we need."

Claire had had scant visits to Edinburgh; on the rare occasions when she came down from Wotan, it was to Glasgow. She found Edinburgh a much more attractive city than Glasgow, and Justin was happy to point out all the relevant places of interest. Justin's abode was in a quiet, historical street near the university. It was in a Victorian stone terrace home divided into four apartments. Inside it reflected Justin's consuming passion, ancient man. The lounge, the apartment's main room, contained bookcases, filing cabinets, and two office desks. It looked like utter chaos; to Justin, everything was in its correct place. This was his workplace. To Claire, it was exciting and filled with interesting paraphernalia. The other rooms were Justin's bedroom, tidy in bachelor fashion, with a small eat-in kitchenette and a bathroom. This was his home.

They walked down the stairs into the rear yard, where Justin's car was under cover in the extended resident carport.

"Young lady, we are going to take a drive to Stirling. It is about fifty minutes up the road."

"Justin, I wish you wouldn't use the term 'young lady.' It is so condescending; it sounds as though I am still one of your students. I am a widow, now involved in a death. This occupies my mind now. Your attempts to divert my attention from this unknown inevitable are not helping. I would appreciate it if we could stay with the reality."

"I am sorry. I must admit to being condescending. I was trying to shield you from what could be a difficult future."

The young effervescent Claire has gone forever. She has become a circumspect adult with the world's weight on her shoulders.

They drove in silence for some time until the interrupted conversation returned. They arrived in

Stirling, drove through the city center, and located Castle Business Park. Everyone knew it. It was new, extensive, and set in a parklike setting that did not exist the last time Justin was in Sterling. The sheriff's offices occupied both levels of one block.

"These are the least threatening legal hearing rooms I have ever seen. I would never have thought that dour old Scotland could move so far into the modern world," Justin said.

"Come on, Claire, let us examine where this inquiry will occur and see if we could sit in on a hearing," he said as he pulled her to him.

"As things get closer, my nervous level is rising," she said.

"The best way to combat those is with knowledge. The scariest is the unknown."

A uniformed man at the inquiry desk informed them they set their hearing for tomorrow morning in room one, on the ground floor next to where they were standing.

"There is a hearing due to start in fifteen minutes. If you are quiet, you can go in and listen," the man said.

"Yes, please," Claire said.

This suited her needs, and she rushed to the door with Justin behind.

"Shush!" said the man.

"Sorry," Claire said as she pried open the heavy door and crept in, with Justin following.

It was a pleasant modern room with a large desk for the judicial officer on an elevated area across the end of the room. At one end of the elevation, was a seating area for witnesses. In front were, in school hall fashion, twenty seats. People, a family grouping had seated themselves, and were now waiting. A notice board informed them it was a hearing on the accidental death of one John

Bartholomew Ryan, age eighty-two, from a fall down the house stairs. Everyone stood up when the clerk commanded it. A middle-aged, suited gentleman entered through a door behind the raised area and sat at the desk.

"My name is Peter Docherty; I will preside over today's proceedings. You may call me 'sir' or 'Mr. Docherty.' We try to keep things informal here. I have several prepared statements before me. I will call the submitters in the order received."

He looked up at the group before him. He focused on an old lady in the front row. She was sitting on one of the small seats and trying to keep balance on her walking frame. This angered him.

"Clerk! It is your role to see to the comfort of all, at my hearings. This is not a criminal jurisdiction; it is a meeting of the bereaved at a hearing of the reason for the passing of their loved one. I will not tolerate disruption to the physical comfort of the disadvantaged here. Get suitable seating for the lady in the front row and have her seated over here to my left, where she will have a full view of our hearing. Madam, please forgive us. Your name? If I may ask."

"Meg Ryan, your worship," she said in an old-fashioned Scottish brogue.

He ignored her ignorance of protocol, a common occurrence at his hearings.

"You are the widow of the deceased?"

"Aye, sir."

"You are the matriarch of this clan?"

"Matriarch?"

"The wisest, most knowledgeable of the people. The head of the clan," he explained.

"Yes, you could say that, although there's not much to beat in our lot."

The slightest sign of a smile lit up his eyes. The security guard returned with a sizable lounge chair purloined from some stuffed shirt's office.

"It would be my pleasure for you to be comfortable. Do you feel up to being able to explain the death of your husband?" Docherty said.

" Yes, I will do that; I am sure you do not want to hear from that lot squabbling like schoolkids. They think they should blame someone or something," She indicated her family group.

"Jack and I have been a pair for nigh on sixty years. From young tads full of life to our slide down the hill to the inevitable. He always was a stubborn man. He fitted the common view of an old Scotsman. His bossy daughters were the worst offenders. He hated the young ones telling him what to do."

"I will not listen to them, never have, never will, and this also goes for you, woman," he would say.

I would mumble under my breath, "Stubborn old fool."

"'What did you say?' he would demand. I would ignore him. We had sixty years of melding. It was a good life. Now he has gone, and I will miss him."

She wiped the corner of one eye and continued.

"I was at the bottom waiting; he wouldn't use the handrails. 'For the infirmed!' he would say."

"He fell, arse over breakfast. He fell hard and was dead. I could see his neck had broken."

"'Dads had a fall!' I shouted, and they came out and here we are today."

She was quiet for a moment, reflecting, then said.

"Peter, could you do something for me? Close this down so we can get on with life."

"In the matter of the deceased John Bartholomew Ryan, this hearing finds 'Accidental death because of a fall.' I declare this matter closed," he said, then picked up his papers, and without another word, left the room.

Claire and Justin sat as the family left. They fussed around the matriarch and were gone.

"What a considerate man," damp-eyed Claire said.

Before they left, Justin asked about Myor's hearing. The clerk searched the court appearance list.

"It was here. They're transferring it to the Sheriff's Court at Viewfield Place. It is easy to find; ask anyone, they all know it. They are expecting quite a crowd. If you must prepare statements for the inquiry, speak to the clerk down there, and he will assist you."

"Change of venue; no problem there. The same procedures will apply. We will go back to my abode, where we will organize your statement and then shop to outfit you in apparel suited to your coming court appearance. You will bet your life that the other side will try to paint you as some type of backwoods hillbilly. Backwoods hillbillys do not wear the type of clothing we will buy," Justin said.

"This is all very worrying, Justin. I thought all you had to do was go to court and tell the story," Claire replied.

"Wrong, my dear. Half of the 'evidence' is in the theatrics that you see in the court. They are there to shape opinions, and opinions are the very essence of verdicts. Over the coming weeks, you will see some performances worthy of the Old Vic. So we are going to visit Jane Davidson, a clothier to my ex-wife June, who shops at the best of the best. So a visit there will sell you a dress to die for, m'Lady," Justin said.

"I'm not one for showing off, Justin."

"Sophisticated is never showing off," he replied.

A visit to Jane Davidson was an eye-opener for them both.

"May I help you?" came from a well-dressed woman.

"Yes, I need a very special outfit for Claire," Justin said as he indicated Claire.

"Oh, I see," she replied. Stunned by Claire's natural beauty,

"You will need to speak to Jean-Claude. He is the man for you. I will summons him." Jean-Claude entered.

"Who is it that requires my attention?"
Then he spotted Claire.

"Oh!" a pause; then, "I have the perfect garment. Last week, we had a fashion show, and their stock is still here. Walk this way," he commanded as he waddled off.

"Here it is, young lady. Made for you; let us try it on," he said.

Claire took the garment to the change room with the well-dressed woman and returned some minutes later doing a smiling pirouette. The green dress swirled and stunned the onlookers.

"Splendid, young lady, splendid! You look the equal or better of last week's mannequins," Jean-Paul exclaimed.

"We'll take it!" Justin exclaimed.

God knows what this will cost.

"It's all too much, Justin," Claire stammered.

"This is the perfect prop for our performance. Persevere, young lady."

On the drive back to Stirling, Justin said, "Well, I now feel relaxed about the Inquiry. How about you?"

"Yes, I also feel more relaxed about it," she replied.

How wrong were they?

Chapter 6

Justin drove into his parking lot, and they went to his apartment, where he selected a clear page of his working diary, sat, and composed Claire's statement.

"You will state everything up to where the harrow fell, and you tried to stop it and damaged your hand. Let the court find out about that business with the knots."

The next day, they drove to the Stirling Sheriff's Court, parked nearby, and walked across to the building. It was impressive, built well over a century ago, and reeked of legal history. With its wide front, the two-level stone building with dormer windows built into the steep slate-tiled roof stood before all. At each end and out of character, were circular towers topped with witches' hats, standing as though they were laughing at the building. The impressive stone entry restored the building to some majesty. They walked into the wooden-floored reception area. With its wide skirting and ornate cornices, it was pure nineteenth century. Here they spoke to the seated clerk.

"Excuse me, could you direct us to the room for the hearing of the accidental death at Wotan?" Justin said.

"Look at the notice board," he said, pointing to the front of the building.

The clerk was not interested in Justin; he was staring at Claire's elegant features and could not stop staring.

She's a one! Wow, is she a looker?

As soon as Justin and Claire left, he picked up the phone, dialed, and spoke.

"It's Doogie from the Sheriff's Court. Could I speak to Editor Bruce? He knows me."

Bruce Ryan was the editor of the *Stirling Herald*, the local newspaper.

"What does that pest want? Put him through."

"Bruce, it might be nuttin', but you've heard of that cult mob from Wotan, up the northwest. They've brought a sizable crowd, with 'em mus' be more than a hundred. They had a killin', and the key witness is the best looker in the world. In my years, I looked at many; in the movies and in the cities; this one is somin' special 'n that bitch Hennessy is hearing it. Wad duya think?"

"Let me have a look, Dougie," Bruce said.

"You will noot forget your old friend now?"

"You'll get what it is worth," Bruce answered. He had a newspaperman's ear for a good story and knew this could be something.

"Who do we have tomorrow morning?" he asked his subeditor.

"George from the front office gets married tomorrow, and everyone in the place is going."

"Blast, we need someone at the courts tomorrow; something could break."

"Chancy; what if nothing happens?" the sub said, then added,

"What about George Caffey's son, Thomas? He is wet behind the ears but as keen as mustard. He thinks he's Jimmy Olsen and you're the chief."

Bruce smiled. "Give him a run and send a photographer with him."

The notice board informed there were four courtrooms in the building, numbers one and two upstairs, three in the basement, and four on the ground floor. The clerk told them their hearing was for 10:00 a.m. tomorrow before Nancy Hennessy, solicitor advocate, in courtroom four. They drove back into Edinburgh, where Justin phoned his solicitor friend Alistair Blare.

"Alistair, who and what is Nancy Hennessy?"

Alistair laughed.

"What trouble have you got yourself into now? Her name in the trade is No-Nonsense-Nancy. Does that tell you enough? Her pet hates are smart-arse males and attractive females. Males because she had nothing to do with them, and the females, if they are averse to Muzz Nancy. You fit the first category. Your associate the second."

"Yes, unfortunately."

"Sorry to be the bearer of such tidings, old son. You stay in touch."

Claire's nervousness and Justin's worry about Nancy Hennessy saw them rise with the sparrows and be at the courthouse at nine thirty. Already the Wotans were gathering. Justin examined the hearing list on the notice board.

This is not the time for socializing. What say we take tea?" Justin said to Claire.

"Yes, please. I am not up to socializing, either," she replied.

They located a small cafe, almost empty, near the courthouse. They sat at a table and ordered tea for two, milk, no sugar. Here they waited, with little conversation between them. Then Justin inquired,

"Nervous?"

"A little; being the center of attention is the worst part," Claire said.

"I will look after you, give short answers, to the point. It is ten to ten. We must be moving," Justin said,

I have terrible vibes about this.

They walked over to the courthouse before 10:00 am. It listed them for the hearing for courtroom one at 10:00 a.m. in the main hearing room. It was at the end of the entrance hall, an ornate high-ceilinged room fitting the courthouse building. It had windows on each side, with the hearing area set out in schoolroom fashion. There was a sizable crowd, Wotan regulars. He looked around. A young man with a notebook in his hand and a large camera around the neck of his teenage offsider alerted him, the press.

What brings them here? Justin thought.

Everybody had entered, and they heard the clerk say, "All stand, please."

They scurried into seats at the room's rear as black-robed Ms. Hennessy arrived. A small, shapeless little woman in her fifties, with short-cropped salt and pepper hair that did nothing to enhance the planeness of her features. She appeared as though she did not like life, and life did not like her. She sat, and the clerk said,

"You may all sit."

As the people resumed their seats, Justin noticed in front the large back of the Reverend, and glimpsed his seating companion, Celena, Myor's mother.

"Claire, I don't want an adverse reaction; Seated together in the front row are Godley, and Myor's mother. Expect tricky moments from those two, especially that snide Godley," Justin said.

"I recognized him and knew she would be here. I am very nervous. If you can, will you move down to the front, where I can see you when I give my statement?" she replied.

"I will be there," he said as he squeezed her arm.

The advocate addressed the court:

"This is not a court of law. Under the Fatal Accidents and Sudden Deaths Inquiry Act, this is an inquiry into the circumstances of Myor Wotan, who died on the property of Claire Wotan in Wotan, Scotland.

"The purpose of the inquiry is for the sheriff—that's me, Advocate Nancy Hennessy—to decide the circumstances of the death."

"The doctors and the police constables' reports on the death will be as stated in the submission. I will call:

Detective Sergeant Edgar Fraser,
Claire Wotan,
Celena Wotan,
Reverend Samual Godley.
All have made written submissions to this inquiry.

I must stress that each of these witnesses I call forward is to give their story of the events as they saw it. Questions to the witnesses from the floor must—I repeat, must— come through me. Comments from the floor will cause expulsion from the court. Note my words on this."

She paused and ran her eyes around the crowd. They remained cowered.

"I cannot help but notice the profusion of the name Wotan in these proceedings. Is it a town or a village? Are all the people in this court named Wotan related? Clerk! Do we have the demographic statistics for Wotan?"

"There is no information available in our records, Your Honor."

"Is nothing up to date in this establishment?"

Justin stood and, from the rear of the room, said,

"May I be of help to the court in this matter?"

"Who are you? Come forward to where I can see you."

Justin went to the front of the court. She glared over her spectacles at him.

Careful here. I will not speak before she addresses me.

"I will ask you again. Who are you?"

"Justin Abbott, Your Honor."

"Name, occupation, and reason for your presence in this court. We are not having a chat. This is an active tribunal." She raised her voice, annoyed at Justin.

"Sorry, Your Honor."

"I am not interested in platitudes. Answer my question!"

Wow! She is like an attack dog in for the kill.

"Justin Abbott, historian, support for Claire Wotan," he said.

Nancy looked around for Claire. "Where is this Claire?"

"She is at the rear of the room," he answered.

"She is the key witness in this hearing. What is she doing there? She should be in the front with the other witnesses. Clerk! Bring that witness forward."

The clerk escorted Claire before "Your Honor."

The Wotans recognized Claire, but not in her current attire. Hennessy waited; then she sighted Claire. A pause. Silence. Another long glance, then she said, "Sit there," pointing to a seat next to Celena. Ashen-faced Claire sat next to Myor's mother.

Please, God, take me back to Wotan, away from this hell.

"Now,"—the advocate paused and consulted her notes—"Mr. Abbott, you may address this tribunal and explain this Wotan place. Is it in the far northwest of Scotland?"

"Yes, Your Honor. If I may indulge the tribunal, my explanation will take fifteen minutes."

"Get on with it, then."

Justin recited the Wotan story. Nobody said a word, and he was careful not to mention any person by name.

"Now the court has some background. As for its accuracy, we do not know. Yet, with this, we will move on," she said.

"I would like to call Detective Sergeant Edgar Fraser." Edgar Fraser sat in the designated witness chair, where he could face the advocate and the public seating.

"I have read your statement and entered it into evidence. Is there any other information that you could add?"

"Yes, Your Honor. I had occasion to speak to Miss Claire Wotan about the circumstances of the death. This upset her as expected, and she began crying. Mr. Abbott attacked me, calling me a callous copper bastard. I realize these situations need utmost tact and, as a detective of twelve years' standing, other people have never addressed me in such a manner. I concluded that this man influenced Miss Claire Wotan and would have been the instigator of any action. This matter needs to be before the courts as a matter of some urgency," Fraser said.

"Thank you, Sergeant; you may resume your seat," Magistrate Hennessy directed.

A murmur ran through the crowd.

You are a callous copper bastard and a vindictive liar, Justin thought.

"Next witness," Hennessy said to the clerk, who called "Claire Wotan."

Justin squeezed her hand as Claire moved forward and sat in the witness chair. All stared.

"I have read your statement. Do you have anything to add?" the magistrate asked without looking up.

"No, Your Honor," Claire replied. The magistrate directed Claire to resume her seat in the front row.

The magistrate looked at the witnesses seated at the front and asked,

"Celena Wotan, do you have anything to add to these proceedings?"

"Yes, Your Honor." Celena, red-eyed from weeping, stood and said, "Myor was my boy. He was not a normal boy. He was mute and could not communicate with most people. That woman there—" she pointed at Claire— "was a married woman who preyed on my boy and seduced him for her carnal pleasure. Her hands are all over his death. That is all I have to say."

With that, she stood and did not resume her seat next to Claire, but retired to the room's rear. The room hushed, and all looked at the flustered Claire on the verge of tears.

Unaware of the room's vibes, Magistrate Hennessy called to the clerk, "Next witness."

They called the Reverend Samual Godley. His presence was imposing. "I entered your statement as evidence. As a man of God, your testament will have weight in these proceedings. Have you anything to add?" Hennessy said.

"I have known Claire all her life; as a young one, she was always outspoken and contrary to the norm. When she was in high school, she would argue with her teachers and always had a contrary opinion. When Mr. Abbott came to our school as a history teacher, he was a clarion of radical ideas. He became Claire's teenage champion; this he played upon, and she became mesmerized by his words. When the full story unfolds, they will reveal him as her Svengali," Godly answered.

Justin angered, rose to his feet, and exclaimed, "I object to this man's insinuations. What right has he to come into this hearing and sprout his biased innuendo? Holy man indeed."

"Order. Order! Mr. Abbott, you will leave this hearing. Clerk, see him out!" the magistrate demanded.

Justin had no option but to leave. Claire looked forlorn as they led Justin from the court.

A heated Nancy Hennessy said, "Claire Wotan, step forward and face me."

A frightened Claire stepped forward and stood facing the magistrate.

"I hold you responsible for the actions of your supporters and if—" Magistrate Hennessy paused.

She had spotted the reporter penciling away with his notebook behind the seated people. Flushed with anger, she rose and pointed through Claire at the reporter and shouted, "Out! Get out of my courthouse now!"

Thinking Nancy directed the tirade at her, Claire raised her hand to speak as she faced the anger. The flash clicked and someone took the photo of Claire, standing and facing Nancy that would project Claire to national prominence.

The magistrate was beside herself with anger and shouted, "I declare this hearing adjourned!" and marched out of the room. The clerk scurried out of the room after the magistrate. Confusion reigned; the crowd stood looking and waiting. Within minutes, the clerk returned.

"Everyone present will receive information about the court's conclusions and the steps required to end the inquiry. We will post a deliberations notice at this office at the commencement of proceedings tomorrow."

Dougie's photo was on its way.

Act One, scene one—not good! Play it up for Claire.

"Typical of the Scottish legal system. Every time, procrastination and delay. Bah! Humbug! Rotten public service. We will go back to my office and get organized," Justin said and began walking back to his car.

They drove in silence until Claire spoke.

"I dislike this, Justin; it makes me nervous."

"I am sure you don't, Claire. What you are witnessing is all the clumsiness of the Scottish legal system, run by lawyers for lawyers."

"That makes me more nervous."

"Look, we will get through tomorrow with Nancy. I know she would make the prime minister nervous, but we must stay the course to the end of these proceedings, and then we will decide what to do. All I can say is chin up. These things all work out okay in the end."

"I hope so. I rely on you, Justin; you are my closest friend."

God don't have me let her down.

It seemed like an eternity to them, but tomorrow came, and "the photo" was out. All the other papers were after the subjects in what will be the "news photo of the year." Krimson Keltic Kween V No-Nonsense-Nancy.

All appeared at 9:00 a.m. at the courthouse, where Justin spied a dark-suited man wearing a cap.

"Officialdom; he will know where we will find Nancy's notice."

"All notices are on the notice board at the end of the hall, governor," he replied.

"This place does not seem friendly today, Justin, and there are so many extra people here," Claire said.

They had not seen the paper with the photo and did not know the news it had generated.

"You look at it that way because you are nervous; come, and we will find out where it is happening. Once we know, you will feel better," Justin said without conviction.

They found the notice on the list.

10:00 a.m. Courtroom Four Inquiry, under the Fatal Accidents and Sudden Deaths Inquiry Act, into the circumstances of the death of Myor Wotan. Finalization Advocate- Nancy-Hennessy.

"There it is. Back to where we were yesterday."

Justin glanced at his watch.

"We have time to have refreshments; we need something to top that scant breakfast," Justin said as he took Claire's hand and headed for the entrance.

"Before we go, I must see someone and get something for this sickness."

"The hospital is down the road; we will duck into emergency and see someone there."

Justin waited and waited until a doctor saw Claire. When she came out, she announced with some trepidation, "I am pregnant."

This shocked Justin, and he had to sit down.

We don't need this now, but we have it. I must appease her.

"That is good news. We will plan our future around the new baby, but first we must get this hearing out of our hair," Justin announced, trying to stay positive and aloof.

"Whose child?

"Myor's."

Justin knew the answer before she said a word, but it still flabbergasted him.

They found a small cafe away from the courthouse, and as they passed a newspaper promo, Justin saw the advertising flyer with Krimson Keltic Kween V No-Nonsense-Nancy and "the photo."

"O my God!" he exclaimed in a despairing voice.

"What's wrong?" Claire asked with concern.

"Yesterday's incident at the courthouse is in all the papers, and those extra people will be from newspapers. You and No-Nonsense-Nancy are a big story."

"What? Show me? Get me a paper," echoed from Claire's despairing voice.

"There is no ducking this; Justin ducked across the road and returned with two papers.

"You're all over them. The reporters will be after you for sure; we will go back to my place and devise tactics." On the trip, Claire examined the articles. On top of everything else, these added to her distraught feelings.

Justin knew Claire could never handle the pressure and would try to lock herself away from the impending problems. Justin consulted several law books and devised a tactic.

"First, you must not make eye contact with anyone you do not know. Then if you must answer, you will say, sorry, I cannot answer you; *the matter* is *sub judice*. The court has the matter, and it is subject to its rules, so we cannot discuss it while it is still pending. So if you are before No-Nonsense-Nancy, that is where the matter stays, and anyone—this includes nosy reporters—will be subject to contempt of court proceedings if anything untoward comes up. Does this make you feel better?"

"Not better, but it gives me an answer. I don't know how much more of this I can take."

"I know the pressure you are under, but once we get the hearing completed, we will be out of here as fast as we can. Come on, chin up; we will get there," Justin said as he took the tearful Claire into his arms.

The gathering crowd took every seat in the public gallery as Justin, and Claire entered. When the crowd noticed Claire, a murmur ran around the room; one shout of Jezebel rang out, signifying to Justin that they were in for a noisy hearing. Seated in the front row were Sergeant Edgar Fraser, the Reverend Godley, and Myor's mother, Celena.

Will she be able to take it?

When they sat, Justin whispered into her ear, "Do not worry about the occasional comment here today. I can tell you without a doubt that there is vigorous support from the Wotans for you; that is all that matters here today. Steel up, focus on the moment, and pause before giving a thoughtful answer. If you are not sure about any point, say so. Do not let No-Nonsense-Nancy fluster you.

The clerk of the court called "All stand" as Advocate Hennessy entered.

"Be seated" followed as the advocate took her position of eminence.

The courtroom hushed as the advocate consulted her notes and addressed the court.

'We have heard the statements from Sergeant Edgar Fraser, a noted practitioner of his calling; the Reverend Samual Godley, a man of God and an eminence in the community; and Celena Wotan, the bereaved mother of the deceased. On hearing their evidence and under the powers vested upon me, I have reached a conclusion on the statements before me. Claire Wotan, you are to face a charge of the manslaughter of Myor Wotan, and if the prosecution reaches the inevitable conclusion, then murder."

Silence.

Then pandemonium; the courtroom was in an uproar.

The clerk of the court shouted, "Silence in the court!" as Advocate Hennessy left the court.

Chapter 7

Claire burst into tears and was inconsolable as the shaken Justin tried to comfort her, to no avail. He stood her up, forced their way through the surrounding onslaught of an existing crowd and hungry reporters, and came face to face with Celina.

"Jezebel! Seducer! My boy was mute, and you preyed on him," Celina said.

They stood apart in silence.

Claire, shocked, with tears in her eyes, cried, "I loved him, and I am with his baby!"

"What! Why the death?" Celina sank to her knees. "This is so messed up. I don't know what to think. How did it happen? Why?" Celina asked.

Flustered, Claire answered, "I don't know how or why."

"Irrespective. To me you now become my boy's mother to be. Together, we will nourish this child."

Claire didn't answer. Justin, also flustered, rang his ex-wife, lawyer June.

"You have done it this time, haven't you? Gather Claire up, get a full transcript of the proceedings, and get yourself down here pronto!" June commanded.

June's offices were in Carleton Place, Glasgow, next to the Sheriff Court. She was practicing through a large law firm, McKinerly and Rothchild. Justin and Claire entered the door of the three-level sandstone building and walked up the stairs, where they confronted the large open-plan office. At the receptionist, Justin asked for June. A young man escorted them to an office in the corner. Justin knocked; a female voice answered, "Yes."

"It's Justin."

"For God's sake, come in! Did you bring all the papers?"

Justin came around the desk and kissed the standing June on the cheek.

"Yes, we have all the papers. They would be hard to miss. You're looking well. Are you still with Robert?"

"No, that's been over for quite a while; I'm married to my work now."

"You must be Claire?" She stood in front of Claire, and they formally shook hands.

"I've been reading the court transcripts, and I will enter a stay of proceedings and get it transferred to next door, so don't worry. These provincials are so wrapped up in their importance."

"I'm busy now, so stay here." She handed a motel card to Justin. "It will take me a few days. So, on your bike, governor, I will see you then."

"Thanks for that; I always knew you were a good woman," Justin said.

"Simply the best, better than all the rest," she crooned as she walked away.

"I am a lot better after seeing June," Claire said.

"Yes, she is tip-top," Justin replied.

When they returned to Justin's room, Claire made a statement that floored Justin.

"I must get away from all of this. There is one thing I want to do, and I am doing it tonight: go to where young people have a good time, on my own!"

Justin knew this was a must in her now rapid development and his answer was "yes."

"But how do you know how to get there and where to go?" Justin asked.

"I will ask a taxi driver; they know everything. You will call me a taxi, won't you?"

"Yes, I will," Justin replied, taken aback.

They had dinner, and the taxi came. Claire had donned "the dress" and looked spectacular.

The taxi driver, an older, well-mannered man, rang the doorbell. Justin opened the door.

"You called a taxi, sir?"

"We did, to the city center," Claire replied.

Claire blew a kiss to Justin, and as she departed, she said, "Don't stay up."

"You be careful now," Justin said.

Claire, angry, replied, "Oh, Justin."

In the taxi, "My name is Reg," said the driver.

"Mine's Claire. I would like you to take me to a place where the young people go."

"How about The Knight Club? All the young people go there."

"Sounds exciting," Claire said.

So Reg dropped Claire at the Knight Club.

"See the shops next to those stairs? Well, up those stairs you go. Here's my card; give me a ring, and I will take you back."

At the top of the stairs, a brown curtain greeted Claire. She pushed through and a large, suited man accosted her and said,

"I am here to keep the riffraff out, but I can see from your attire that you aren't riffraff, so in you go."

Claire pushed through another curtain and was in The Knight Club. It was as modern as tomorrow. She sidled up to the bar that occupied one wall of the room.

Wow!

"What's your fancy, miss?" the bow-tied man asked, gesturing to the wall of bottles.

Claire pondered, then answered, "I will have a Coke, please."

As quick as a flash, a tumbler of ice and a small bottle of Coke stood in front of her.

"That will be three pounds twenty, miss."

Claire paid for the drink and enjoyed the fancy presentation, although the price surprised her.

"You are the lady from the papers?" the barman asked.

"Yes, I'm trying to forget that; it's why I am here tonight," Claire said,

"Oh ho, here we go, heaven's gift to humankind, the master of the universe, himself," the bartender said.

Claire looked up; approaching them was a big blond man in his twenties.

"The Keltic Kween, a night out? I'm Jack; fancy a dance?"

Claire knew all the dance steps from school and wanted to be in "it." Her answer was, "Yes, please."

So Jack and Claire danced and danced until Claire asked,

"Can we have a break? My feet are hurting."

"Why not? We will get something to drink." Jack said.

They reverted to the bar. "What is your poison?" Jack asked.

"Something not as mundane as a Coke; one of those fancy drinks?" Claire said.

"I know the thing, I'll order a scotch and ice, and for you, a brandy and Butter Scotch schnapps on ice," Jack said.

"You sure? I am not sure about these things." Claire said.

The barman looked at him, "A scotch and ice and a brandy and Butter Scotch schnapps on ice? Your usual and a Leg O'Pen-ere?" The bartender laughed.

"Yes, and keep them coming," Jack said.

The long glass and the tinkling of ice with two measures from the array of bottles on the wall were all Claire saw.

The sweet, cold taste was pleasant to Claire, and she gulped it down.

"Whoo, take it slow," Jack said.

"Well, I will buy another," Claire said.

Jack attracted the barman. "Another for Claire, please."

The barman placed another drink before Claire.

"Slow this time," Jack said.

"I was thirsty," Claire said.

One more drink and she could sense her world spinning.

"I better go now. I'm drunk, but I cannot go to Justin like this," Claire slurred.

"You can come to my place and rest for a while; it's down the road," Jack said.

"Oh, thank you, Jack," Claire said.

Jack, the seducer, was all smiles as he basked in the trap he had set.

The best looker in Scotland. I cannot wait.

A taxi was in front of The Knight Club, and Jack hailed it and bundled Claire through the rear door.

"Where to, governor?" the driver asked as Jack sat beside him. He mumbled an address as the taxi set off.

"Your girlfriend looks under the weather; she won't be sick in my car, will she?"

"No, she's fine," lied Jack.

They drove a short distance to a squat block of old flats in suburbia.

"Anywhere here," Jack said.

Jack struggled to get Claire out of the taxi, up the stairs, and then to his apartment at the rear. He had his key in his hand, let Claire in, and followed her to his bedroom, where she collapsed in slumber. Jack left her, went to his kitchen, opened his fridge, and had a large swig from an open wine bottle. He struggled Claire out of her dress and threw it on the floor, then went to his bathroom and showered. Jack dried and buck naked, went to his bedroom and slid in beside the sleeping Claire, who didn't wake until she felt his hand on her vagina. Claire screamed as Jack clamped his hand over her mouth.

"Shut up, you bitch, or I will hit you real hard," Jack snarled.

He tore at her underwear as he slapped her hard across her cheek. Beaten, Claire lay still and crying, submitting to her humiliation.

When he exhausted his lust and lay still next to Claire, she attacked his eyes, her fingernails scratching down his cheeks.

"Fuck you, you bitch!" Jack screamed as he punched her hard, high on the cheek.

"Get out of my house now!" he yelled as he threw her clothes in her face.

That taxi man—his card.

She rummaged in her handbag and found it,

Reg Simpson. Taxi Service. All Hours.

Claire dressed and headed down the stairs and out the door into the pitch dark. She could see the lights of a service station down the road and headed toward it. It was an all-night station that serviced the taxi industry. There were two taxis out the front, and she showed the card. A driver looked at it and said, "Reg is off till tomorrow. Is it urgent?"

"Yes, I've got to get home."

Claire told the man the motel's name where she was staying. "I know it. Hop in; you look as though you need a lift."

The drive took a few minutes and dropped Claire at the motel's Porte Cochere.

"That's a freebie. You look like you need one," the driver said.

Claire walked in and knocked on their door. Justin opened the door.
"What happened? Look at you." Tears, tears, buckets of tears as Justin held her and let it run its course.
"Come in; we'll have a cup of tea, and you can tell me all about it. It's the middle of the night, you know," Justin said.

Justin made tea.
"Tell me all about it," he said.
"He raped me."
"What! Who did this?"
"Jack."
"Jack who?"
"Jack I don't know."
"The police will want more than that," Justin said.
"No police! No police: I couldn't stand it," Claire exclaimed.
Perplexed, Justin said,
"Come on. We will go to bed and sort it out in the morning."

They woke at first light. Justin was up before Claire and made tea and toast for two before she arose. As they supped their tea, Justin said,
"What's this no police business?"
"Do you realize how stressful this press business is? I want out now! What do you think will happen when this is all over the papers?" Claire said.
"I see, yes, I see. But this bastard is not getting away with it. I promise you that," Justin said.
"Oh, I forgot, I received a message from June. She wants you to come to her office and see Mary and go

through your court proceedings documents. It will take about three hours. I'm excluded, as I'm a time waster. So do your hair in a bun, wear a cap and jeans. That will do, whatever. Not the dress, though," Justin said.

"Okay. Where will I see you?"

"Back here at the motel. I will come back here," Justin said.

Justin wanted some free time to research this John character.

He went to The Knight Club, which was a somber place in the daytime, with a few staff around.

"Yeah, I remember her. Good looker, red hair. She went with that smart arse, Big Jack. She had a couple and was a new drinker drunk. That bastard does it all the time. Someone needs to shorten him up."

"She is a Wotan," Justin said.

"Oh-oh, then he's in big trouble. There's a lot of Wotans around here," the barman said.

"Where do I find them?" Justin said.

"You will find some of them at The Rugby Club. They are good at that rough stuff," the barman said.

Justin found The Thistle Rugby Club and entered. There were a couple of drinkers and a barman who told Justin, "The footballers are down in the gym."

Justin went down to the gym, where there was a group of men on gym machines.

"Any of you men know Claire Wotan?" Justin asked.

"Yes, yeah, the red hair?" Various answers came back.

"Do you know a big, blond man called Jack?" Justin asked.

A mumble of affirmatives greeted Justin.

"Well, last night, that bastard raped Claire," Justin said.

A group rumble of anger filled the room. A voice called,

"Has she called the cops?"

"You know all the publicity about her and the courts. It had crushed her, and she couldn't stand the cops and press milling around her. She wants to get out of the place and back to Wotan. As a favor to Claire, do you men think you could sort it out?" Justin added.

"It will be my pleasure," said a brute that had arms like tree trunks. His associate said, "And mine, I know that smart arse bastard, he hangs around The Knight Club picking up young fluff."

"I've heard the stories. We'll handle it every time we see the prick," said the second man.

"Smartarse will have to leave town pronto, or he will live in the casualty ward," Another added

Justin was sure the rugby fellows would look after Jack McDunn, and they did the next day. Jack purchased the newspapers to take home to see if there was any mention of last night. His research revealed nothing. Then a knock on the door.

"Coming," he answered and opened the door. Before he could react, two burly figures bundled him back into the room.

"We're Wotans and we're here to speak to you about Claire. Do you know her?"

"No" came from his mouth as he swung a roundhouse right fist. A cocked elbow blocked this. Then, in a flash, an open heel of his assailant's hand drove under and upward, forcing Jack's nose backward into his face.

Jack sank to the floor, not knocked down, but slumped with a bloody, broken, numb nose. "We'll be back tomorrow, next week, or anywhere we see you. Sayonara, you prick!"

As quick as they came, they were gone.

"Oh shit, the pain!"

What to do? Go to the hospital and get my nose fixed. I will go to London for a while and plan for my future. They won't be there, or will they? Bugger, bugger, fuck the Wotans.

Justin arrived at the motel as Claire turned up. "June said they will fix it up without going to court. Good news, aye?"

"Great news," Justin said.

"How did you get on?" Claire asked.

"Attended a couple of matters that needed clearing up. Pretty boring," Justin replied.

In two days, June read the transcript and emailed Justin, in which she wrote, Reverend Jonathan Godley: info, please! I'll look after that dope Frazer.

She also messaged Frederick Mackenzie. "John Godley. Info required. He is from Wotan."

June knew Frazer. He was famous for submitting evidence that reflected his feelings, not the facts, and in two court cases, she had torn his evidence to shreds.

June then made an appointment with the clerk of the court at Glasgow.

Frederick Mackenzie had the nickname "Freddie the Ferret," of which he was proud. By nature, he would search all the nooks and crannies and chat with all "in the know" people; he was the "go to" man for anything or anyone. If he did not know, he would find it; if he could not find it, he would invent it. Freddie was an invaluable asset to certain types of people. Those in the information business, such as newspapers, and those in the snooping business, such as certain legal people, were his staple diet; anyone that would pay his sometimes exorbitant fees (*a man's got to eat, you know.*) were his customers. He was a small man and always wore an over-the-eyes fedora. He looked his nickname.

From her contacts, lawyer June gave two names: The

Right Reverend Jonathan Keith Godley and the New Calvin Kirks of Scotland.

His brief: Something is wrong here; find everything.

Freddie went to work. The web told him that the New Calvin Kirks' premises were just out of Glasgow, so Freddie went down for a look. He found it easy enough and could drive right around what looked like a medieval fort. He went into the nearest tavern and had an ale and a chat with the barman.

"Funny building over there, that one with the high walls."

"The nunnery? Yes, they used to cloister themselves away from us hairy beasts to be with Jesus. Anyway, Jesus left; you cannot blame him; everyone leaves Glasgow whenever they can. So if Jesus left, so did the nuns. They ran out of recruits at the time of the First World War. It was vacant and dropping into disrepair until the present people gained it some years back. It is now a home for orphans or wayward boys run by the New Calvin Church. There are dark whispers here. Creepy damn place if you ask me."

All Freddie said was, "That is interesting. You find these buildings with a tale to tell all over the country."

A pause. "While you were at it, I will have one more ale, then get out of your hair."

If life were always that easy,

'Now how to find out about that Godley person without him knowing anyone is looking or inquiring?" Freddy pondered.

Freddie had an acquaintance at the *Daily Clarion* in Glasgow; Bert Longly was his name. A long, long time ago he was a chatty reporter, but now he is a battle-hardened, cynical subeditor.

"What are you ringing me about, Ferret, you little pest? Last time you rang, you took from me, and I did not receive; piss off."

"Wait, wait. Do not hang up. I have a lead to the biggest story to hit this town since the war, and you will have an exclusive. It's linked to the Keltic Kween."

This hooked Longly, and the Ferret knew it.

"See me at Aunties at five o'clock," Longly said as he hung up.

Aunties was a typical English tavern; small, cozy, and built for the community. It was not the *Clarion*'s local, but a pub off the beaten track of the newspaper people. They had one ale when Bert said, "Come on, spit it out; I am a busy man."

"Do you know of the Reverend Keith Godley?"

"I do; the police want to speak to him; pedophilia. Serious stuff. He vanished.

The people at his monastery, if that's what it is, do not know or will not say; they are all under a cloud. The whole thing is being hushed up. Brian Thurston, the local MP, has something to do with it. You know him, everyone does, with his tartified wife. Well, what's this big story that you must tell?"

"I know how and where to find him," the Ferret said.

"Who?" Longly asked.

" Jonathan Godley."

"Wow! That is a BIG story. I can see the banner headline:

"*Clarion* Exclusive: Pedophile Priest Exposed,"

"Where! Where is he?"

"He is at Wotan. He's the local churchman,"

"Wotan?"

"Right up the western coast of Scotland, in never, ever land. We need to knock on the door of that monastery."

"'We' doesn't include you, Ferret."

"Wait, wait. The local head office of the church is not up there. It is at that old monastery at Maidstone in Kent."

"I owe you. The office will fix you up," Longly said.

"Good; I'm off now. I have other matters to investigate," the Ferret said.

Longly returned to the newspaper and co-opted his senior reporter, Jake Webster.

"Jake, I want you to knock on the door of that abbey and say that you wish to contact the Reverend Keith Godley."

"The cops want him?" Jake asked.

"Yes, but we know where he is, up at Wotan. This knock is a fishing expedition," Longly said.

"Wotan ah! The Keltic Kween. Do you reckon it's a big story?" Jake asked.

"The biggest," Longly replied.

Jake went to the nunnery, located the entry alcove, and knocked and knocked.
An old cleric opened a speaking hole in the door and answered.

"Patience is a virtue, young man. What can I do for you?"

"My name is Jake Webster from the *Clarion*. I wish to speak to the Reverend Jonathan Godley."

"There is nobody here with that name." He slammed the little door.

"Thank you for your kindness," voiced Jake.

Inside the abbey, the cleric informed the Right Reverend Thomas Edwin Cole, the self-anointed bishop of the New Calvin Kirks of Scotland, of the inquiries for Jonathan Godley.

"That Godley is about to interrupt our plans; summons him to appear before me with haste."

When Godley received the message, he was ashen.

The word is out, the police, the press, gossip, or some sinister group about my promised status.

Godley planned to go to Glasgow and make Oliver McGinty responsible for the day-to-day affairs of Wotan while he was away.

He was a worried man and thought through the probable reasons for going to Glasgow as the train traveled on its boring journey. Godley caught a taxi to the abbey, knocked on the door, and the old man answered.

"Come in, we have expected you. The bishop is waiting."

The pair shuffled, at the old man's pace, along passages until a large door confronted them. Godley knew it well, and he felt a nervous tightness in his chest as the old man knocked.

"Come in."

Godley knew the voice as he opened the door. The old bishop in full regalia confronted him.

"Well, it's out in all the newspapers; they are knocking on the door. What do you say to that?"

"An unfortunate set of circumstances, dear leader," Godley said.

"One man's folly, yours, could doom us all. Leave me now and I will think this through. We will all finish up in prison for a long time if this is not sorted out. Speak to me in the morning; use your usual room. No one is in there now," the bishop said as he dialed a number.

"Brian Thurston, please." He waited and "Brian Thurston here," answered him.

"The press is around and Godley's here," Richard Cole answered.

"A combination that could blow our secret to smithereens. I better get down there," Thurston said.

"And I will get a couple of security guards down there ASAP."

Thurston arrived as the security service pulled up. "I'm Brian Thurston. Guard this door. Nobody is to come in unless Cole says so. He's the boss."

Thurston hurried inside to Cole's room and confronted Cole, "I've paid you plenty to keep our disabled son hidden and you have blown it, You have extorted a small fortune from me. Your usual 'I will need an advance to keep the word from getting out' is bloody extortion. Get Godley out of here late at night so that nobody sees you. It might blow over."

But Godley had other ideas; he was in the chapel, musing.

Cole will excommunicate me, which will mean that I am no longer a "chosen one" and the gates of Heaven will shut for me, and I could finish in prison for a long time as a pedophile.

Godley looked up into the steeple and the bell tower.

The answer is up there.

He left the pews and climbed the steep spiral stairs into the choir stalls. Here he could see the stairs up the spire to the bell tower, Godley climbed the narrow spiral. He found what he wanted. Anchored on a steel ring and coiled on the floor was an old bell rope. He threw the coil of bell rope down to the choir stalls. He hurried down the stairs to the rope and dangled the end over the rail. It ended three meters from the floor.

"Perfect!"

Godley took several attempts to tie his noose, which he placed over his head. He moved forward to the choir stalls rail, sat on it, and dangled his legs over.

"I am coming to you, O Lord," he said as he launched himself into oblivion.

A slight pause three meters from the floor. Then the rope tightened, his neck stretched, eyes bulged, and as the death shudders settled, his sphincter muscles relaxed and the contents of his bladder and bowels let go and dripped onto the floor. The death sight of the Right Reverend was not a pretty one.

It was Cole who found him. He was down at the chapel for his morning prayers.

The sight shocked him. He shuddered and let out a muffled cry.

Cover it up or the world will know. But how? I can't get him down.

Godley's feet were at eye height.

"The bastard did this on purpose. He thought he was an 'elect,' the fool, and when I said I'd get around to throwing him out, he thought he would be for fire and brimstone instead of the pearly gates. Now I am left with this mess to sort out," Cole said.

Get Thurston involved.

Cole rang Thurston, who answered, "Big trouble here," and hung up.

Cole looked up and saw Brother Gibbons.

"I've called the police," Gibbons said.

"You what?" Cole said.

"Yes, and an ambulance, to see if they can help with the Reverend Godley. May Heaven help his poor soul."

"Watch things here for a moment and do not do or call anybody or anything!"

Cole rushed to his office to call Thurston, but too late, sirens in the distance, then heavy knocking on the door. Cole ran to the door and opened the viewing hole. All he could see was a police identification folder.

"Police! Open the door."

Cole's brain was whirring.

Play it soft and gentle.

Cole opened the door to reveal the police and Thurston.

"What seems to be the trouble, officer?"

"I am Sergeant Clough. We've here about a death," he said.

"Do you have the right place? I am Brian Thurston, the local member. It is a most respectable institution run by the New Calvin Church."

"That may be so, but our orders are to go in and check, so in we go," Clough said.

On reflex, Thurston made the silliest mistake of his life. He grabbed Clough's arm.

The second officer moved forward and restrained Thurston.

"You are under arrest for assaulting a police officer," he said as he cuffed Thurston's wrists.

"Come with me," he said as he led Thurston to the police car, where he radioed for help. Within minutes, police car sirens were in the distance.

In no time, the place was swarming with blue uniforms, some concentrated on Godley's body; others searched every nook and cranny of the monastery. The story was out. The hiding of cruel treatment of the disabled for financial gain was there to see via the swarming press. They gathered some big names of clients of the institution. Gossip. Press. Rumors, oh! The shame of it all.

Chapter 8

It was in all the papers: "Cleric Suicides." June's brain was ticking. "It's clearer now."

When she arrived at her office, she rang the clerk of the courts at Glasgow.

"Jim, have you read the newspapers?"
"The suicide?"
"Yes, his name is Godley. Ring a bell?"
"Should it?"
"The Claire Wotan matter," June said.
"Ah, yes," the clerk of the court said.

"Well. we should have a stay of proceedings, Celina Wotan has withdrawn, and police officer Frazer's evidence is not worth tuppence. Now, without Godley, there is nothing," Joan said.

'I agree with you Joan, but no case, no legal fees." He laughed.

"Bugger off, you cheeky public servant," Joan replied.

It was a formal solicitor letter Claire received.
"Read this, Justin. We can go home at last!" excited Claire yelled.

"At last!" Justin exclaimed, then added,

"We must thank Joan, and then get onto the bus to Kinlochbervie. We will be back at Wotan in no time."

Justin made a telephone call to Joan's firm to book an appointment to pay for the account.

"Tomorrow, nine in the morning, so we better be up," Justin said.

Joan greeted them. "What? You pay. I thought you wanted a freebie. Richard!" she commanded her junior. "Dig out the expenses on the Wotan matter, and he will pay." She pointed to Justin.

Justin paid and said, "You are my very best legal eagle."

"Pay and stay away. All this stuff is clogging the works." she said as she disappeared.

The train trip was boring, but the boat was exciting for Claire. All the crew were communicative, "Where have you been?" "Haven't seen you in a while." "Welcome back." Dr. Brodie was on the boat, and his eyes lit up in recognition.

"Claire, Justin, how are your tribulations? Got them sorted out?"

"All sorted out by Justin's ex-wife June, she works for a law firm in Glasgow," Claire said.

The doctor looked at Claire's stomach; she was showing her pregnancy, which Dr. Brodie recognized. "As soon as you settle in, you better come and see me to check you out and see that everything is going all right."

"I would like that, doctor. It's Myor's child," Claire said.

"All the more reason," the doctor replied.

The boat was maneuvering into its dock. Claire could see her parents, Oscar, and Rhonda, standing with Celina, and this confused her. Has Celina told them?

"Welcome home," the group said in unison.

"Don't tell us now. Wait till we get home to tell us; we'll go to my house and have a cupper. I know where everything is." So off they trudged. Five of them squeezed into the small eat-in kitchen.

"Tell us everything, Claire."

"There is so much, and everything happened so quick. Could you tell them, Justin?" Claire said.

Justin realized Claire's mind was foggy. "Sure thing," answered Justin, and spent the next hour explaining everything and answering questions. Except the rape.

"That's the story, more like an odyssey, but our girl survived it," Justin said.

"My baby is the first thing. I must see Dr. Brodie. I will wander around and say hello and then get into my house and garden," Claire said.

Justin and Claire walked over to her house. The grounds and her gardens were unkempt and when she opened the house door, a stale smell greeted them.

"We must get the windows open and get some fresh air in," Claire said.

When they came back to the kitchen, Justin said, "We need to have a chat where we can talk in private. You're home now, with a new life ahead of you. What part do I play in that life?" Justin asked.

"What? I love you; I thought we were going to live together in my house," Claire said.

"That's okay, but what am I going to do?" Justin asked.

"You will do as you want. I'm not dictating to you," Claire said.

"Tomorrow I am going to my office. There will be a pile of mail there. I will come back in the next day or two, depending on circumstances," Justin said.

What I want is time to think of the future, my future.

Justin went to his office in Edinburgh. His secretary wasn't there, but a pile of correspondence was. He spent some time sorting things out. When he finished, he sat and thought things through.

I will speak to Blair. He is a level-headed person.

With his lifelong friend Blair Docherty, he could speak and receive sound advice. Blair, a doctor, suggested he make the appointment with his secretary for tomorrow.

His surgery in Edinburgh was a composite type, where he shared rooms with a group of doctors.

There was a mixed bag of patients waiting, but Blair called him within a few minutes.

"What brings you here instead of the local pub?" Blair asked. "You sick?"

"No; I want some advice on matters of the heart, I am seeing a teenager, and I don't know where it is going, I am infatuated with her, and she is talking of a lifetime relationship. That's scary." Justin said.

"Is this that Claire girl? Are you mad? Well, it should scare you. My daughter is that age and she doesn't have a brain in her head. Think of the future. What are you going to do when she is gallivanting around? You cannot act like a parent, you know," Blair said.

"That's not all. She's pregnant," Justin said.

"To you?" Incredulous, Blair gasped.

"No. To Myor; he's mute."

"Is he the one that the harrow killed?" Blair asked.

"Yes."

"Was Claire charged with that?" Blair asked.

"Yes, she was, but not convicted, because of lack of evidence,

"Did you think she did it?"

Justin paused in his thoughts.

"Yes, I do, but she regretted it after."

"Justin, I thought you were in Wotan to expand your knowledge of your pet theories on the development of man, and Claire was a test case."

"True, but I became infatuated with her and her need for help," Justin said.

"There is an old saying 'There is no fool like an old fool.'"

"In retrospect you are correct, like an old fool. I couldn't see it," Justin answered.

Then he added, "I'll go back and finish my work, and the relationship with Claire will be teacher and student;

thanks for your help; I knew if I discussed it with you, I would reach a logical conclusion."

Justin went back to Wotan and met with Claire at the house.

"Well, young lady, how have things been?"

"A group of us Wotans went to Glasgow last night; we had the best time," Claire said.

"You went where? You know what happened last time you went wandering down there?" Alarmed, Justin said,

"We were all right; Bruce looked after me, and a group of young men and women went; we didn't come home till the next morning; a lot were too drunk," Claire said.

"Where did you stay?" Justin asked.

"Everywhere. Some stayed up drinking all night at the Kinlochbervie wharf. Bruce knew a small hotel where we stayed."

This makes my decisions easier.

"Claire, I had to make some lifestyle decisions and went to see my old friend and doctor Brian Docherty. He reminded me of my station in life and the differences in our ages. I am more than twice your age, and for all that palaver on the other night, even though you had the time of your life, I couldn't be in that; I am too old, like your parents. We should face reality and come to another arrangement other than what you are expecting."

"I thought you loved me," Claire, distressed, said.

"I do as a father loves his teenage daughter," Justin said.

"I'm a castoff here, am I?" Claire said, then burst into tears.

Crocodile tears.

Claire stood, didn't look at Justin, and walked out, leaving Justin seated and alone.

After a minute, Justin went to the kitchen window and saw Claire in her back garden, weeding between the vegetables. He walked out and joined her, and they weeded for quite a while when he said,

"This is thirsty work, I'll get us a drink," and left Claire to go to the kitchen.

When Justin came out with two fizzy drinks, Claire was on a bench seat with her back against the wall. She took a drink and didn't say a word. Justin sat next to her, and they finished their drinks.

She is playing no-speaks, Justin thought. *Well, I will play schoolteacher.*

"I am here to help you, for no other reason, and if you don't acknowledge my presence, I will leave you and be on the first boat out of here in the morning," he said and then shouted, "Do you hear me?!" and walked inside with the drink glasses.

Claire burst into tears.

Justin looked out of the window, as she was still crying.

Real tears this time.

Justin let her emotions weep out, then sat beside her.

"Feel better now?" he asked.

"No, worse," she said.

"Come inside, and we will have a chat and sort things out," Justin said.

Justin took her hand and led her inside, and they sat at the kitchen table.

"Have you heard of libido? Justin asked.

"Sort of, in my readings, but it makes little sense. Why are we talking about this?" Claire replied.

"Because it's important. Your libido makes you want to have sex. Your libido is natural and comes when you reach puberty. Libido is at its highest when you are young. As you get older, it declines until, in old age, it disappears altogether. This is natural. When you are young, you copulate and have children. This is how humanity has survived.

"Remember in school, our classes on Homo sapiens. For hundreds of thousands of years, they followed the same course.

"When we age, this urge reduces little by little and we desire sex less and less. If we were to be lovers, you would be as frustrated as you were before Myor came into your life, and try as l might, I wouldn't be able to perform to meet your expectations. You would be a resentful and frustrated lady, or you would stray, and then I would be a resentful old man. Not a pretty picture, is it?" Justin said.

"Not when you put it like that, but that wouldn't be with us," Claire replied.

"You have the baby, then we will talk some more. But be happy. This will be the biggest moment in your life, bar none!" Justin said.

"I have had bad thoughts about having the baby. There's the father, Myor; not family material, and I have been having bad dreams."

"Bad dreams?" Justin asked.

"Have you read *Rosemary's Baby*? The father of her baby was the devil. With Myor, the devil is around," Claire said.

"I saw the movie, but that's fiction, a fabrication of someone's mind. It's not real. I'm not good at babies, but if you see Doc Brodie, he will give you some books to read. He's here tomorrow, isn't he?" Justin said.

"Yes. I'll book in now," Claire said.

Claire saw Dr. Brodie. He examined her, sounded her stomach with his stethoscope, took her blood pressure, and announced, "You're fine, we'll get an ultrasound and a blood test in Kinlochbervie, so you will have to go in there tomorrow."

"Doctor, I must tell you about *Rosemary's Baby*," Claire said.

"Who? I don't know any Rosemary," the doctor said.

"No, not a person, a book."

"Oh, yes, I remember now, the movie from long ago. What about it?" the doctor said.

"I have read it. She thought she was having a baby with the devil. Well, with Myor and all, these things ran through my mind," Claire said.

"Tommyrot! What are you doing reading that rubbish? Go to the library when you are in Kinlochbervie and see Heather. Say I sent you and borrow some birthing books. And speak to some new mothers and mothers to be, move into that circle. Among me, you, and the gatepost, your baby will be fine. See you after the ultrasound comes back."

Claire came out of the doctor's office with a skip in her step and a song in her heart.

"I've got an all-clear, and I have to go to Kinlochbervie tomorrow for a blood test and an ultrasound; then I will have the picture of my baby," smiling Claire said to Justin.

Claire went to Kinlochbervie for the scan and pathology and was happy with the procedures; she returned to Wotan to wait for the results of the tests and her picture of her baby. Dr. Brodie returned with the scans, and there was the baby curled inside its mother's womb. She was ecstatic and took the scan wherever she went. Doc had seen the signs and kept his mouth shut, to his eternal guilt. Claire was the talk of the town, and it filled her life with happiness.

From time to time, libido raised its head, but she had no time or energy for such preoccupations. The coming baby was her preoccupation.

Claire sat with Justin at her kitchen table chatting about anything and everything, when Claire felt the moisture between her legs.

"My waters have broken," she cried.

"What do we do now?!" Justin yelled as he rushed to Claire.

"Into that bedroom," he said, as he carried, lifted, and dragged Claire to the bed and lifted her on it. He rushed to the door and shouted,

"It's coming!" half the village heard.

"I'm on my way," said Mary the midwife, from a few doors away.

"Get out of here Justin, and boil some water, you hopeless male," Mary said.

It was a small baby, and it was all over in a short time. Mary lifted the baby by the ankles and a short sharp slap to the rear, had the mite emitting a little squark. She wrapped the baby and handed the bundle to Claire. Claire, exhausted and covered with sweat from her ordeal, accepted her bundle. As she looked, the baby glared at her with a distorted Myor face. There wasn't a movement from the almond eyes. They looked through her as though she didn't exist. Justin entered the room and heard and saw it all.

Mongoloid.

Claire looked into the baby's eyes.

"You are going to haunt me all my life for what I've done to you, but I've done no wrong. You were not even a Wotan. Get out of my life now!" Claire's message went to the baby, but it was to Myor, and Justin knew so.

"Get that hate out of your heart and face your responsibilities. You are not a girl anymore, you are a mother, so be like a mother. Life goes on." Justin demanded.

"I'm off," Justin was out the door to book a seat on *Esmeralda* to Kinlochbervie.

I'll leave her alone till she faces the realities of life.
With Wotans, there are no places for challenged offspring.

At Kinlochbervie, he purchased a return bus ticket to Edinburgh and sat and thought over the situation.

Claire, as a single mother, won't cope with that child. She relied on Myor a lot more than she thinks, and the enormity of her crime must hit home.

Irrespective of the Wotan problems, Justin had office business to attend to, and people to see, which would take a couple of days. This side of his life was fallow, with his undivided attention being on Claire. There was not enough time for other things.

His apartment was a mess, so first thing he tidied up and took his washing bag to the laundry and made his bed, then motored over to his office. He let himself in and went to the desk, where there was a note from Mary. She has family problems and will be away for a few weeks. For the rest of the day, he read his mail and made phone calls to all and sundry. One letter of interest gave him a laugh. It was from the Department of Education offering the position of part-time teacher of history at Wotan Senior School; they enclosed an application form, which he completed and sent in. The sun was setting when he left the office.

"I will be a good social gentleman and go to the pub for dinner," he decided.

He met Barney, the publican, who organized a meal and a beer and left him to his devices, which were meeting, greeting, and drinking; hangover-type drinking.

He slept in the next day, but he could not get his imagined responsibility for Claire out of his mind as he meandered around town.

I've got to go back before she does something she will regret.

The bus took him to Kinlochbervie, where he waited for the ferry. In case she did not need him at Wotan, he booked a room at a small inn, then spent the next hour in a cafe with a long black coffee. *Esmeralda* was at the wharf loading goods for Wotan. He waited until they sorted the deck clutter out and then spoke to the deckhand.

"How long, Jimmy?" He knew the boy from his classes in the school, who answered with,

"About half an hour."

"Your wife and baby will be glad to see you, sir."

"Well, we hope so," Justin said.

Your stupidity got you here. Now use your brains to get out.

The seas were mild, and the trip pleasant, but as Wotan came closer, his chest tension increased. There was no welcoming committee as he disembarked and headed into the settlement. One old resident passed him and ignored his presence.

The welcome mat has gone.

He walked over to the house. The door was open, so he knocked, no reply. Justin walked in and took the door to the right. There was Claire, bending over the baby's change table. He could see the little bundle. He was aghast at what he saw. Claire was holding a cushion over the baby's face. Claire swung around, saw Justin, and spoke. "He's not breathing."

Justin saw the lifeless body, raced to the back door, and shouted,

"Help! The baby's not breathing!"

Justin knew that Wotan tradition dictates there is no place for those who cannot live independently. It is difficult to know when this is being used as a connivance.

The first to arrive was midwife Joan, who, without saying a word, rushed to the baby, put her ear to the little chest, then started two-finger resuscitation. She looked at Justin and said,

"Hey, useless, get the doctor. He is around town somewhere."

Justin was glad of a reprieve and was out the door in a flash.

"Has anyone seen Dr. Brodie, urgent, the baby?!" he yelled in a town crier's voice.

The message went around the town like a flash, and Dr. Brodie appeared with his bag of tricks. He was no sooner through the door with his stethoscope in his ears, and its diaphragm on the baby's chest under Joan's hands. The doctor placed his hand on the baby's forehead. He looked at the edgy Claire.

"When did this happen?"

Justin started to speak.

"I didn't ask you, let Claire answer," the doctor snapped.

"Ten minutes ago," Claire answered.

"You can stop, Joan, the baby's gone," he said and added, "Claire, you can do one thing, go to the kirk and arrange the burial. I will fix the death certificate. Then tell Celina, you haven't been near her at all since the trials. I'm not happy about these circumstances." Then he swung to Justin, "I hope your conscience is clean because mine is troubled."

With that, the doctor packed his bag and was out the door.

The word was quickly around the community, and gossip was rife.

Chapter 9

Justin moved back into the house, but they both avoided discussing the baby's death, even though they knew the truth. Justin, in his musings, knew Claire was a true Wotan, and she was true to the tribe's ethos. He accompanied her to see the new Reverend, who was a disciple of a "God forgives, so forgive everyone" type of religion. Justin thought of him as a wimp, but better than Godley. The Reverend invited them into his office behind the kirk.

"What can I do for you young couple today?" the Reverend said.

"We would like to arrange a quiet burial for my newborn son," Claire said.

"Not a funeral?"

"No, a burial at the cemetery," Claire replied.

"Yes, I have heard about your sad situation. Being newborn and not Christian changes the parameters somewhat. I will arrange for the burial as soon as possible. Oh, there is a small fee. And a small donation for the poor will help God's work," the pastor said.

"Yes. That will be no problem," Justin replied.

The pastor placed a small box in the grave and said a few words. Nobody attended except Claire's mother, and that was that. Another sordid chapter closed in Claire's life.

For a few weeks, everything was quiet in their life. The students accepted Justin into the school to teach history and mathematics. Joan Hobbs, re-conscripted to the school, was his boss. He was on her wavelength, and they were the best of friends.

They disbanded the trifecta of the Village/School/Church Council and asked Justin to be on the Village Council, which he accepted. They had long since shown Godley's lackeys the door.

The word was around that Wotan had the best fishing on the coast, and keen anglers came from all over to try their luck on the weekends. They would bring their tents; their fishing gear; and, of course, their alcohol. Wotan didn't have a retailer for alcohol, and an amount of beer was always in the anglers' coolers. As a result, they set up camp where it suited them; took the space they wanted; and at night were a mob of noisy drunks. It upset the locals, and they turned to the head of the Village Council, Justin, to provide relief.

Justin looked at the internet registry of old titles in the land register; nothing. A trip to Glasgow to the Scotland land register didn't enlighten him. The total area was open space. He went to see his solicitor friend Alister Blaire.

"I searched the Sasine register, which is the register of ancient titles; nothing. They deemed all that area around Wotan open space," Alister said.

"Wotan doesn't exist?" Justin asked.

"Not on official records; nobody registered it. That is not unusual, not in the rural areas, anyway. These come up from time to time," Alister said.

"Well, it is about time it happened. We'll do it," Justin said.

"I have an idea. See your local member, George Hedley, make an offer he can't refuse, and get him to work for you."

"But I don't have any Mafia status," Justin said.

"No, but you can be the Godfather." Alister laughed at their banter. "Hedley is behind in the polls and with an election coming up, he needs all the votes he can get. How many votes in Wotan?"

"I see, I see. Well, Hedley must have a Godfather visit, mustn't he?" Justin replied. "But before I go, what sort of title do I want?"

"Out there, I would suggest a company title, so everyone owns it," Alister said.

Justin made an appointment to see George Hedley in his office in Aberdeen.

"What can I do for you, sir?" George said.

"I understand your elections are coming up?" Justin asked.

"Yes, and very important, too, since that pretty boy turned up and is running. All the women think he is beautiful," said George.

"What say you if I could offer hundreds and hundreds of votes? What could you do with them?" Justin asked.

"Well, they could save my political life," George said.

"Have you heard of Wotan?"

"A bit, but not much."

"Well, they are in your electorate; get somebody up there and have them all enrolled, and I will guarantee they will vote for you provided you back Wotan's needs."
Justin said.

"I should know," said George. "As Grandpa used to say, nothin' fer nothin'."

"Before the election, they want you to get company title on that land. The Wotans have been there for thousands of years, and now some smarty pants are upsetting them. I have some papers to bring you up to speed on Wotan," Justin said, and handed George the papers from Joan and Edwin Wotan.

"These will tell you about Wotan. Could you read them before you go? You will catch the boat from Kinlochbervie, and when you land at Wotan, go to the store and speak to Beryl McNabb. She will tell you where to go and whom to see. I am a schoolteacher there. One other thing; We need a mobile phone tower. There is no reception at Wotan now," Justin concluded.

"So far, so good," Justin mumbled as he left.

George Hedley was quick off the mark and, in two days, was at Wotan with a surveyor and a council enrollment officer to complete their tasks. It was like lightning, for a public service job; they finished in no time. BT was also there to survey for the phone tower.

Justin went back to the house to see Claire. Like all late teen people, they had their groups and socialized wherever, or at Inverness night spots that were full of young people wandering from venue to venue, especially on the weekends. From Kinlochbervie, they had their cars in the Wotan parking area, and in groups, they went on their merry way. Coming home was different; being young people, going home was the last thing on their minds, and each would make their arrangements. As the ferry left early on Saturday evening, they would stay wherever. This was a worrying time for the parents, worrying about unwanted pregnancies for their daughters or fights for their sons. Most of the parents had spent their youth in Inverness as reminders.

Justin wasn't a parent, but had their worries. He knew Claire's gift of gab was her protector, but her beauty made her a magnet for all the young males on the make. He knew he could not express his concerns, as she would clam up. So whenever she came home, she would prattle about the happenings, and he would ask his appropriate questions.

At one time, she mentioned Dougal.

"You know Dougal from school?" Claire said.

Justin knew Dougal. He was a gangling youth, short of manhood by a couple of years, and popular with the students and teachers.

"Ah, yes, very good at math, our young Dougal," Justin replied.

"I danced with him. He is cute, and I spent the night with him at the club. I also stayed with him; he is crude, like most young men. I wanted to meet Dougal next week, but his girlfriend, Anna, a local from Inverness, will return from London; she is down there for a wedding," Claire said.

"It sounds like you had a good time. Let's hope you can get together again, as you never know what tomorrow holds," Justin said.

"I hope so," Claire replied.

At a council meeting, they discussed a frequent complaint, the casual anglers' behavior, and the increasing aggressive, retaliatory behavior of the Wotans.

"Someone is going to get hurt," Counselor Hurley said.

"We need a police officer," said another counselor.

"I concur. I will speak to George Hedley; he still owes us a few favors," Justin said.

When told of the situation, George said, "The best thing to do is get a recruit at Wotan, one of your people; he can go to Glasgow to train to be a police officer. I will speak to the powers to be for training, then I will arrange for him to transfer to Wotan," George said.

"That's a great idea, George; you're more than a pretty face," Justin said.

In the village, they gave a stocky young man the nickname "Dobber" at school for obvious reasons. The council would approach him to see if he would like the job. Everyone said he would be perfect, and he was. He accepted the position and went to Glasgow for training and, within six months, was home in Wotan and on the beat.

In the town was a centuries-old two-room brick building that had been the settlement's jail. It now stood without a floor and a roof.

"No problem, I will bring the timber up on *Esmeralda*," Jim, a wharf hand and local handyperson said from the dock. It seemed like no time at all before a police officer and his jail were operational. Now a night with Dobber was enough to quiet the most uncooperative angler.

Claire, morbid and circumspect about the Myor incident, didn't associate with her peers until Justin intervened.

"The only person who will snap you out of your present mood is you, nobody else!" said Justin in his best schoolmaster's voice.

"Keep going to Inverness on Saturday nights. You might meet someone who will take your mind off Myor," Justin added.

"I'm sure Dougal will be there and want to dance with me, sweep me up in his arms, and hold me tight," Claire said.

"What about his girlfriend?" Justin said.

"Well, what about her? She is not a Wotan, you know? She's from Inverness," Claire answered.

"Whether she's a Wotan or from Inverness is of no consequence. You be careful," Justin said.

"Oh, for God's sake, Justin, don't you think I can handle the situation?" Claire said.

"Well, I hope so. Have a good night, and I will see you tomorrow," Justin answered.

Claire left home so she could have the earliest ride to Inverness, and arranged a lift with two men she knew from school. They commandeered an appropriate gasoline fee from her. But the driver was a ratbag who took unnecessary risks. All Claire could do was sit with her heart in her mouth and vow never again. They dropped her at her preferred night spot and headed to their bar, where the beer was cheap.

The doorman gave her a nod of recognition as she sauntered in. She was in her favorite green dress. The room had a few arrivals, and the band was setting up as Claire spotted her imagined adversary. She was sitting in her dark-haired onlyness at a booth. They made unsmiling eye contact, and instead of slinking away, Claire headed for her.

"Are you waiting for Dougal, my dancing partner? If so, I will join you," Claire said as she sat down uninvited.

"Piss off, you Wotan slut, you're not getting my man," Anna seethed.

"Fuck you, slut. I'm sitting here," Claire seethed back.

It happened in an instant. Anna yanked at Claire's hair as she screwed Claire's face. Claire's reactions were reciprocal. They were like two hens fighting over a roosting place. The bouncer was on to them as Dougal entered; he saw the altercation and ran away like a frightened rooster.

"Out, you two," the bouncer said as he collared the women and escorted them out into the night. "You go that way," he said to Claire, "and "you go the other," he said to Anna. "Now!" he shouted, "or I will call the cops!"

Their dander had subsided, and they felt foolish. They knew they had lost both the fight and the man. Claire, not knowing what to do, went to a rooms-to-let establishment she knew and sobbed the night away.

Claire was on the first ferry back to Wotan. Last night and today, her thoughts were on Anna, evil thoughts.

"You're home early; how did it go last night?" Justin asked as Claire entered their abode.

"She had me thrown out of the night spot; I'll throw her out of my life. She humiliated me in front of Dougal. It will be all around Wotan, the shame of it all," Claire replied, and began crying.

Justin sat beside her, placed his arm around her shoulders, and waited for the sobs to stop.

"Whoa, slower; tell me what happened," Justin asked.

"I went to the club to find Dougal. He wasn't there, but that dark-headed woman after him was, so I went to wait for him. She called me a bitch and told me to fuck off. Well, I told her to fuck off, and then she tried to pull my hair, and I pulled hers, and the bouncer came over and threw us out of the club. All this was going on as Dougal came into the club and saw us; some other Wotan people were in the club as this was going on. I feel ashamed."

"Do you know I have never seen women fighting? Have you?" Justin asked.

"Not since school I haven't," Claire said.

"You must have been like a pair of Banshees, and as for that language, pure fishwives, shame on you both," Justin said.

"She started it," Claire explained.

"What are you, still a schoolkid? Because you are acting like one. It's about time you grew up. See this Anna person and sort it out like an adult," Justin said.

Claire stood and said to Justin,

"I'm going for a walk; I need time to sort it out."

As she went for a walk, she headed up the back of the property to where she had her sexual encounter. A dream? Or with Myor? Her inner thoughts cascaded through her head.

Justin is not a Wotan and does not understand; he is one of them and supports Anna, an outsider. Tribal practice demands I, Claire, rid the world of Anna, irrespective of what the outside law says, so that I can claim Dougal. It will have to be an accident. I will play it smoothly until the occasion arrives.

With that decided, Claire went back to Justin.
"I've decided; I will ignore Anna and get on with my life. My garden is a mess again, and I miss the income from it. About the incident, I won't mention it; if anyone does, I will say she attacked me. After all, she did, and her being non-Wotan will be enough explanation. If we ignore each other, that will be all right. What do you think?"

"That sounds all right; if it suits you, then it is okay," Justin said.

She is not leveling with me. She is not forgetting about Anna; her Wotan get-even instincts are too strong. I better watch out for anything and everything.

Claire went to work in her garden, and Dougal volunteered as her helper. It was on his initiative, as he needed some cash, and jobs were scarce in and out of Wotan. Dougal's father told him, "Any port in a storm."

The items Claire grew were in demand in Wotan, and it needed two people to plant and reap the root vegetables. Dougal still mentioned Anna in their conversations without being aware of Claire's raw nerves. When there was an occasion, he rubbed bodies to keep their erotic thoughts running, Claire noticed.

Claire still frequented the night spots in Inverness, but dodging Anna was a major problem. It was best for her when Anna was away, which was frequent, and then Dougal was Claire's. This situation persevered for quite a few weeks until a window of opportunity opened for Claire, and she used it. She was on the Kinlochbervie ferry, which was operating on its busy timetable; it was Christmas and the best time for young people to have fun. The weather was freezing; the seas were rough, and the wind blew sleet off the ocean. She was glad when Kinlochbervie wharf's floodlights were in sight; there was Dougal with Anna, waiting. Claire guessed Dougal was going home for Christmas with the family, and Anna was seeing Dougal off. Anna had difficulty with her umbrella, which had blown inside out in the wind.

Claire knew the boat's passengers would alight at Kinlochbervie, and those returning would board without delay. The boat could then return to Wotan before the weather closed the run down. Claire had minimum time to plan her action and left her group to sprint down to the cargo hold, where she could alight unseen through the lower cargo ramp. At the cargo hold, a deckhand stood before her.

"Upstairs to alight, miss," he said.

"Oh, the boy upstairs said I could get off here," Claire said.

"Did he, now? Well, he is not very bright. Okay, out you go, but mind your step."

Chapter 10

Claire alighted and scurried behind some cargo containers. The boat left with Dougal on board, and Anna stood at the edge in her full-length coat. The wharf hands had scurried to their shelter. Anna was alone at the edge of the wharf, fighting with her umbrella. Claire's approach was silent and quick, and with a push on the back, she tumbled Anna into the pitch-dark sea. Claire looked down at the floundering Anna, with the spread of the overcoat supporting her less and less as it became saturated. As with most in the area, Anna was a poor swimmer, and as the coat absorbed water and aided by her heavy soaked boots, she disappeared. Claire stood watching to ensure she had disappeared, then ran to the shed to raise the alarm. Claire shouted,

"Quick, come; a woman has fallen off the wharf!"

Panicked, the harbormaster and his assistant rushed out onto the wharf.

"Where?!" he shouted to Claire.

"Over there," said Claire, pointing to the spot. The three of them rushed over to where Anna had vanished.

Sitting some fifty meters across the water, parked under the trees on the edge of the water, was the Bentley limousine of financier Edward Gilbert, who was canoodling with Alice Jones. Mrs. Gilbert and Sergeant of Police Alec Jones were not aware of their spouses' tête-à-tête.

"Did you see that? That woman pushed the one in the blue overcoat into the water," Alice said with concern.

Edward Gilbert had the Bentley into reverse and swinging around and out as he said, "I saw nothing; I wasn't there; negative publicity will break my company and me. We should put our association on hold for the moment."

The harbormaster climbed down the fixed wharf ladder.

"There's nuttin' down here." As he rose to the top, he said,

"Smiffy, run along, the tides goin' out, she might be in th' drift."

Smithy ran, watching the water to the end of the wharf. Then he shouted, "Nuffin, boss!"

"Well, get inta th' office an' call the cops."

Alice expressed her concern on the drive. "What about the incident at the wharf?" she asked.

"I've never been there. Never! Understand, never. Here is your car. No contact, please."

Alice was home by eight. Her husband was still working the night shift. She couldn't sleep; the incident worry kept her awake.

I will have to tell him everything about Edward and me. "As you sow, so shall you reap." There's no hiding now, it will be out for all to see.

Alec had the morning papers when he arrived.

"We had an incident at the wharf last night. A young lady fell into the water and drowned," He said.

He threw the paper down in front of her. "Read that," he said.

Alice read the article. "DEATH AT THE WHARF. Anna Burgess of Inverness had a fall from the ferry wharf at Kinlochbervie and drowned despite the heroic actions of Claire Wotan, who tried to prevent the fall."

"I could see her stumble, but she fell in despite my effort to save her. She was a poor swimmer, as I am, and I could only watch as she disappeared under the water. I called for help, and the harbormaster and his assistant came and called the police," Claire Wotan said.

Alice looked at her husband and said, "Is it your case?"

"I know about it. Why?"

"It wasn't an accident. She pushed her, and I saw it," Alice said.

"What?! How do you know? What are you doing about it? Have you called the police?" Alec said.

"No, I thought about it all night. I must tell you the complete story first," Alice said.

"Last night I said I was going to a church meeting. That was a lie; I am living a lie. When we originally got married, it filled me with optimism for starting a family, but nothing worked out. Then, out of the blue, Mr. Flash Car Gilbert propositioned me. Me, of all people. He flattered and attracted me. I went with him in his car down by the quay, and this is where we saw the murder," Alice said.

"I know about that prick, Gilbert. You are not the only stupid fool that has hopped in his car. I'm calling this in; time is of the essence in murder cases."

He dialed. "Jacki, it's Alec. Put me through to detectives."

A male voice answered. "Cole here."

"It's Alec here, Reg. Who's working?"

"Most are on holidays, being the festive season. Important?"

"How's murder sound?" Alec said.

"That important, aye? How about McMillan and King?" Reg replied.

"Send them around to my place now."

"What have you done, belted the neighbor?"

"Smartarse!"

Alec hung up and confronted Alice.

"I hope you know what you are getting yourself into. There is no turning back or changing your story. Be careful with your answers and hide nothing, not the slightest detail; it will all come out, newspapers will be around, the neighborhood will be full of gossip, and you will be in it for the long haul. The wheels of justice turn slow in Scotland," said Alec.

"Do I have your support after what I told you about me?" Alice asked.

"Yes, until this is over, then we will look at things," Alec said.

"I am so sorry, Alec; I am so foolish," Alice said.

A knock on the door and Alec shouted, "Coming!"

Two men in suits confronted him.

"You look so obvious," Alec said. You're Ken McMillan. I've seen you around, and you must be John King. Come in."

"Evening, Sergeant," they said in unison.

"Come and meet my wife, Alice."

After the pleasantries, the four sat at the kitchen table. "I am an observer here; I will not utter a word. Ask what you may," Alec said.

Although nervous at first with the sergeant present, they soon fell into their routine. They were meticulous and polite, although Alice was tense talking about Edward Gilbert and their affair.

"We will talk to Mr. Gilbert when we leave here," said Detective McMillan.

The two completed their interrogation, refused drinks, and were on their way.

"The ball has rolled, and God knows where it will stop," Alec said.

When the officers knocked on the door of the Gilberts, Edward Gilbert answered.

"What are you people doing here?" he asked.

"We are asking about the death of Anna Burgess and thought you might help us," King said.

"I was never there," Gilbert said, with his wife behind him.

"Never where? sir," McMillan said.

"I was at a local bingo game," Gilbert said. His wife looked at him.

Bloody liar, I was there, and you were not.

The detectives returned to the station.

"What do you do with the record of that liar?" King asked McMillan.

"Put it in the L file," McMillan replied.

They filed their reports and were told to bring Claire Wotan in.

Their inquiries on how to get to Wotan prompted the universal answer, "Get the ferry." The detectives were lucky, *Esmeralda* was operating on Christmas timetable, so they had no trouble getting there and back on the same day. When they arrived at the Wotan wharf, they asked at Beryl McNabb's store about where they would find Claire Wotan.

"Up at that brown house; Claire and her man live there. He says he isn't her man, but everyone knows," Beryl said.

The two protectors-of-the-state walked past the vegetable garden, saw the door open, and knocked on the jamb; a male voice answered, "Come in."

They walked into the eat-in kitchen, where two people were washing potatoes in a huge tin dish.

"What can we do for you gentlemen?" Justin asked. "We are getting a crop ready for market."

"We're looking for Claire Wotan," McMillan said.

"That's me," Claire said.

"We're arresting you for the murder of Anna Burgess," King said.

"What?" cried Justin.

"These warrants have irrefutable evidence, sir."

Miss Wotan, will you come with us? If you refuse, we will take you in handcuffs," McMillan said.

Justin knew there was no maneuvering room.

That story she told me didn't add up; why was she hanging around the wharf when the rest of her group was on their way to Inverness?

"Come on, Claire; we will go to court and appeal this matter," and then to the police officers,

"Do you think those handcuffs are necessary?"

"It is the procedure," the police officer replied.

"The community here is a weird mob; they're very clannish, and if anything is happening to one of theirs, watch out. You could have a riot on your hands, and you could be in the middle of it," Justin said.

"In this case, we could leave them off around here, but they must go on when we get to Kinlochbervie," King said as he looked at McMillan for approval.

"I'll have to go with her; I am her legal representative and must be with her," Justin said.

"That's okay, but what about the ferry?" McMillan said.

"There's no Christmas timetable; it keeps going. We will have to wait," Justin replied.

The wait was brief; nobody got off, and a couple of late shoppers came on board. The wind and rain had abated, and the trip was pleasant.

Claire snuggled up to Justin, wanting to be a part of him. She wanted him to own her and her immediate problems.

"When the police on the death of Anna came, there were no handcuffs then?" Justin said.

"No, everything was amicable," Claire said.

"Well, something else changes their mind. Rack your mind for info because someone has given contrary information, somewhere or somehow. Have you spoken to anybody?" Justin asked.

"No and no, nobody or nothing. One other thing: will you tell Mum and Dad? I don't want them hearing things through scuttlebutt." Claire said.

"What happens when we get to Kinlochbervie?" Justin asked the police officer.

"There will be a Black Mariah to take Claire to the holding cells in Aberdeen; you can go to the courts there to apply for bail," said McMillan.

"How do you get out of Kinlochbervie?" Justin asked.

"We'll get a lift with Claire," the police officer said.

"What about me?" Justin asked.

A plaintive cry from Claire of "Justin" heightened his awareness.

"Shanks pony, old mate," McMillan replied.

As Aberdeen is on the east coast, Justin's first thought was,

I must get my car, then go to Aberdeen.

He went to the bus terminal in Kinlochbervie and bought a ticket to Edinburgh, to leave in forty-five minutes. He phoned his office, informing them he would be there later today. The bus trip had two features: boring and long. He reached Edinburgh, caught a taxi home, had a snack, rang his ex-wife, June, then drove to Aberdeen and Claire.

The holding cells were in a pleasant modern building, not as suspected; a blood house full of drunks, and the staff were polite and helpful. As the case was one of A-says-this against B-says-that, irrespective of its severity, the Aberdeen Sheriff's Court granted bail.

"As the charge is murder, the case will be in the High Court of Justiciary at a place and time to be announced," the clerk said.

"Well, that's that," Claire said as she gave Justin a hello hug.

The voice of confident youth.

"Don't get ahead of yourself, young lady; the game has not even started," Justin said.

Justin dialed June's phone.

Chapter 11

"I've been expecting your call; you and your girlfriend have moved up to First Division, right into the High Court of Judiciary. If you are asking for help, count me out. That place is out of my league. Get your pencil and write this down: Giles, Tobin, and Partners, ask for Samual Tobin, and tell them I told you to call. When you call, they will attempt to pass you off to some underling, but insist you want Tobin. They are in Edinburgh. You will find them."

Justin and Claire drove from Aberdeen to Kinlochbervie and Ted's parking, and Justin took Claire up onto the wharf to the scene of the accident with Anna.

"I don't want to be here. Let's go home," Claire said.

"You cannot avoid this. It's for your life. This is all there is, unless you want to spend the rest of your life in prison," Justin said.

This shocked Claire; from then, she was subservient to his wants and answered all his questions about Anna's death, but from her point of view.

They returned to their abode, and Claire tried to be normal, but it was always there, her Sword of Damocles. Their first stop was seeing Dobber, as he was in the eyes of the court, their representative.

"I've received correspondence about your matter; come to my lockup each day, and I will fill in the form; you are my first customer for this type of thing," Dobber said.

Claire agreed to follow his wishes and was acquiescent to any directions.

From there, they returned to a quieter version of life. As everybody wanted to know everything about the happenings, and word was spreading like wildfire, they stayed home as much as possible.

"Let the rumors spread; the truth will come out soon enough," Justin said.

They tended the garden, and their old customers came back.

"You are so much cheaper than the shops at Kinlochbervie," was the common saying.

At the first chance, Justin phoned Samual Tobin and made an appointment for three days. He didn't take Claire, as he thought she couldn't leave Wotan.

"No, no, she can come; we are court officers and part of the court," Samual told him as they sat down. Jonathan, balding, was about Justin's age.

"Tell me about this matter; I gather you know Claire's story?" Samual said.

"Are you aware this matter went to the police about five days ago, and they accepted her word about the events? She walked out a free woman and a hero for trying to save the same woman," Justin said.

"Yes, I read that in the papers," Samual replied.

"Here is a document that Joan Wotan, a clan member, gave me. I would like you to read it; it gives a feel for the place," Justin explained.

"Yes, I would appreciate that," Samual said.

Justin handed an envelope that held the document to Jonathan. "That is my copy, so I would like it back. It was a thesis Joan Wotan, one of the more intellectual Wotan residents, wrote about the history of Wotan."

"You will have it back at our next meeting, when I will meet Claire," Samual said.

"The Wotans have been a closed society for a thousand years at least and have values and rules that have passed over the generations. Extreme suspicions and even violence were their first reactions to any interlopers. For a quiet life, they have agreed to abide by our laws, but find them difficult over killing outsiders; killing outsiders has always been part of their law," Justin said.

"This sets different parameters over the whole matter, and I would like to discuss the case among my peers; in fact, we may need outside experts. I will be in constant contact with you," Samual said as he ushered Justin out of the office.

Within a few days, Samual was back in contact.

"We have done extensive research within the Scottish sphere of influence. According to Blackstone (1842), Scottish law will apply, but courts should respect all local covenants. So any trial, including Claire's, must have the respect of the courts on the matter. This could mean nothing or carry considerable weight. The way we will know is by the trial judge's rulings, or it could be grounds for appeal. The research shows that Claire Wotan appeared before Stirling Sheriff's Court, which referred her on the charge of murder. By the way, your young lady generated an amount of press publicity; remember *Krimson Keltic Kqueen v. No Nonsense Nancy*. You will expect the same when the word is out?" Samual said.

"That charge wasn't applicable and should not have been there. An examination of the evidence had the matter thrown out; the publicity came from a newspaper stunt with a fluke photo. We will handle the press. We are getting to be old hands at this," Justin answered. They made an appointment the following day with Samual where he could meet Claire and discuss tactics.

It was a few days after, and it came in an official envelope from the High Court of Judiciary, via Dobber. It was a summons for Claire Wotan to attend the High Court of Judiciary at 1 Mare Street, Glasgow, in Court 1 on the 10th of March, at 10:00 a.m. before The Right

Honorable Lord Anthony, Lord Justice General of Scotland, to answer the charge of murder.

The time had come, and both Justin and Claire felt the shiver of the unknown.

Justin rang Samual, who said,

"It's happening in three weeks. The High Court clerk has contacted me as the defense advocate. The High Court clerk is questioning whether the court has authority over Wotan Law. This case could be precedent-setting because the Wotans were there before Scotland existed. The people of the court won't get much sleep this month, and poor old Anthony, a reasonable old fellow, will pull the hair out of his wig. I must be at the court the day before the trial before we get into the nitty-gritty."

"Another thing that may interest you. Nancy Kerrigan is the prosecuting lawyer. You know her?"

"No-Nonsense-Nancy, yes, we know her. Do we ever?" Justin said.

"Well, my directions to Claire are to get that hair cut modern and short and be in a smart blue suit. Appearance is significant in front of the judge and that large jury. She must look like a smart young businesswoman, not a victim," Samual said.

Justin turned to Claire. "No-Nonsense-Nancy is the prosecuting lawyer assisting the judge, and because of this, you are to change your appearance to a businesswoman."

"Oh, no, Heaven help us," Claire pleaded. The news overwhelmed her, and she cried. Justin put his arms around her and let her emotions peter out.

"Remember, we have Samual to speak for us and Nancy is for the court. All you must do is answer the questions, and Nancy must ask them. This is not run under Nancy's Tammany rules. This is the highest court in the land. These bastards will not beat us. We'll see who is laughing at the end. Steel up, and let's go get them." His words of encouragement lifted her spirits.

I hope I can keep her up until it is over.

The stress of tomorrow made life difficult. The word was out, and the rumormongers were out and about.

"You should show your parents the summons and give them some ammunition to look after themselves. You can also let the clan know you're not afraid to show yourself. This trial is not all about you; Wotan law existed thousands of years ago, and your trial is about this so-called murder. Even if it was true, it is being tried under Scottish laws, and Scotland didn't exist when Wotans came here," Justin said.

Clair felt invigorated after Justin's lecture and was more than willing to spread the word. She visited her parents and showed them the summons, then told them about Justin's ideas about the conflict of the laws. This prompted a "how dare they?" attitude, and her pa was so angry he was going to man the barricades; he withdrew his antique pistol from its oilcloth and assembled it on the table.

"Put that thing away, Pa. You're not in Dad's army. We are going to court, where Jonathan, our legal man, is fighting, not us," Claire said.

"I hope so," Pa answered.

The Judiciary Building in Glasgow was of centuries-old sandstone construction in Greek Revival style. Six fluted Doric columns supported its portico, giving a judicial majesty to the entire edifice. Escorted by Dobber and Justin, Claire entered, followed by a phalanx of

Wotans; they fronted the administration desk, and Dobber presented his summons papers.

"You've brought an enormous crowd; looks like half the supporters of the Glasgow Rangers," the clerk said.

"Naw, the supporters of Claire and the Wotans," Dobber replied.

"Don't know them. Second Division are they?" the clerk replied.

Dobber ignored him and read,

"Claire Wotan, charge, murder: High Court of Judiciary."

"Yes, here you are. You're our major trial here today, Court 1, straight ahead. The Right Honorable Lord Anthony, Lord Justice General, at 10:00 a.m.

"You are early, but you can sit in there and wait; see the clerk of the court. He will let you in. I don't know about the followers, though, but it's his problem."

They did as directed, and the Wotans followed. Justin expected a centuries-old walnut-paneled room, except the décor was as modern as tomorrow. The Wotans had taken all available seating and were waiting for the proceedings to begin, like at kirk.

The Lord Justice General watched the courthouse through his monitor in his chambers.

"Tell me, Philby, who are those people sitting there?" the judge said to his aide.

"They're Wotans supporting the accused; they are a benign group, Your Honor," the aide said.

"If they are disruptive, I will clear the court. They are waiting for my decision on whether the court recognizes Wotan law. This causes some difficulty; I have researched the subject in English records, where they have dealt with indigenous people in their colonies for centuries, and their approach will apply here today. The trial will be under Scottish law, with all reasonable consideration to verbal Wotan law."

"Yes, Your Honor. There is another minor problem: it has come to light today that our advocate deputy, Ms. Hennessy, heard a Sherriff's Court hearing where she recommended a murder charge; our defendant was also the defendant in that case. A huge amount of publicity there," the aide said.

"Yes, I remember it now, *Krimson Keltic Kween v. No Nonsense Nancy*. I'll have to answer a murder charge if some people around here don't become organized; I could abort the trial over this nonsense. Get Hennessy in here, now!" the judge said.

The aide knocked on the adjoining room door.

"Ms. Hennessy, the judge wants to see you now; he's steamy, to say the least," the aide said.

A worried Hennessy entered the room,

"Yes, Your Honor."

"These courts are in big political trouble over their expenses. How much do you think an aborted trial and a retrial cost the taxpayer?" asked the judge.

"I don't know, Your Honor," Hennessy said.

"Well, look it up because your actions have almost caused the canceling of today's trial. Why didn't you disqualify yourself?" asked the judge.

"I didn't think it mattered."

"You didn't think it mattered! Let me tell you, if you display any animosity or make a show of yourself, or if I must abort the trial, you will see if it mattered. Get yourself ready for court; they will call us soon," the judge demanded.

"All stand." All stood for Right Honorable Lord Justice General Anthony in all his regalia to move to the bench and sit.

"You may sit now," said the clerk of the court. All sat.

The jury of fifteen people shuffled in; their eyes were on Claire sitting before them: the accused with her security blanket, Samual Tobin.

"This court is now in session to hear the charge of murder against the accused, Claire Wotan of Wotan, Scotland."

Samual said, "One moment, Your Honor. Are the charges to be heard under Wotan law or Scottish law?"

"I have given much scholarship to this question, and this trial will be under Scottish law with careful consideration of Wotan laws and customs."

"Thank you, Your Honor." Samual resumed his seat and whispered to Claire,

"This question, if at all, will apply to sentencing."

"The court calls Claire Wotan." Claire rose and entered the stand.

Nancy (No-Nonsense-Nancy) was in front of Claire (the Krimson Keltic Kween). A pregnant pause fell over the court. It all flashed back to both.

"Could the advocate proceed?"

"I thought there would be moments," mused the judge.

"On the night of the twenty-third of December, could you describe to the court what you saw as *Esmeralda* approached the wharf at Kinlochbervie?" Nancy asked Claire.

"They illuminated the whole wharf with floodlights. It was cold, the wind was blowing the rain, and waiting at the wharf to catch the ferry was Dougal, returning to Wotan," Claire replied.

"Anybody else on the wharf?" Nancy asked.

"Yes, Anna, seeing Dougal off," Claire replied.

"Who is Anna, a Wotan?" Nancy asked.

"She is not a Wotan. She is from Inverness," Claire replied.

"Do you know her?" Nancy asked.

"Over the past few weeks. We are not friends," Claire replied.

"Not friends? Being thrown out of a nightclub for fighting, how about bitter enemies?" Nancy inquired.

"That was nothing, a few cross words," Claire answered.

"Do your feelings about Dougal, a Wotan, I hear, going out with Anna, play any part in this altercation?"

"A little, she started it," Claire said.

"You would say that, wouldn't you?" Nancy stated the obvious.

"Advocate!" came from the judge.

"I withdraw the statement," said the advocate.

"Tell the court what happened after the boat arrived at the wharf," Nancy said.

"We all got off and arranged lifts to Aberdeen. This is where I saw Anna having trouble with her umbrella. The wind had blown it inside out, and she was having trouble with it at the wharf's edge. I rushed over to help her, but she tumbled into the water before I could grab her," Claire said.

"I ran to the harbormaster's office and called for help; they searched along and under but could not find any trace of her," Claire said.

"On the evidence I have, I would like to suggest a different scenario," the advocate said. "When *Esmeralda* was arriving, you spied Anna on the wharf. At this point, you enacted your plan. You hurried down to the lower goods storage deck and met two boat employees who questioned your presence. You ignored their directions to return to the main deck to disembark; instead, you exited through the cargo hold on the lower deck, where you could conceal yourself among the cargo crates on the wharf until your moment arrived. *Esmeralda* had departed as Anna waved goodbye to Dougal. This was the moment. Anna was at the wharf's edge where her umbrella had blown over the edge. She stood there looking down; you hurried from behind and gave her a two-handed push in the back; over she went and into the water. Her wool overcoat and heavy waterproof boots held her afloat for a couple of seconds; then she departed from this life," the advocate said in triumph.

"No! That's not true. The police investigated this, and they exonerated me of it; I tried to save Anna," Claire said.

"I would like to excuse Claire Wotan and call Alice Jones to the stand," Nancy said.

Alice Jones was a fortyish suburbanite who sat before Nancy.

"Mrs. Jones, could you tell the court where you were at the time of Anna Burgess's death?" Nancy said.

"I was sitting in a car across the quay from the floodlit wharf," Alice said.

"What did you see?" Nancy said.

"I saw a woman push another woman off the wharf and into the water," Alice said.

"Could you identify that woman?" Nancy said.

"It was the accused; the accused said in the newspaper she was there and tried to rescue the deceased. She didn't help the woman. She pushed her in," Alice said.

"That is all, Your Honor," Nancy said.

Samual rose and approached the witness.

"It was raining, and the wind was blowing. Correct?" Samual asked.

"Yes," Alice said.

"I have been to the council offices; the distance from where you sat in a car is forty-five meters to the wharf.

That is almost half the distance of a football field. You were sitting in a car in the rain; is this correct?" Samual asked.

"Yes, the car is a new Bentley. We had the motor running to keep us warm, and the windscreen wipers come on automatic when they get wet," Alice said.

Samual asked, "In cars, the wipers clear in strokes and pause with each stroke. At the commencement of the stroke, the rain covered the window. Could it have been at one of these cycles that you thought you saw a push that was momentary?"

"No, I saw it."

"Is the car yours?" Samual asked.

"It is the property of an acquaintance," Alice answered.

"Was the acquaintance with you?" Samual asked.

"Yes, he is the car's owner," Alice answered.

"What is his name?" Samual asked.

"Edward Gilbert," Alice answered.

"What were you two doing on this dark and stormy night?" Samual asked.

A pause.

"Answer the question," the judge ordered.

"Being nice to one other," Alice sheepishly answered.

"I should imagine, as you say, 'being nice' is all-consuming. How did you drag yourself away from being nice to look at the wharf forty-five meters away?" Samual asked.

"It was right in front of us; we had to see it," Alice answered.

"What attracted you to the wharf?" Samual asked.

"One woman pushed another into the water," Alice answered.

"What did you do then?" Samual asked.

"I said to Gilbert, 'That woman pushed the other in,'" Alice answered.

"What did he say?" Samual asked.

"I was never here." He answered as he reversed the car out, drove away, and then dropped me off at my car as he said, 'I don't wish to see you again.'"

"You went to the police?" Samual asked.

"I didn't know what to do, so I went home to wait for my husband; he's a police officer," Alice answered.

'Wait'? What does 'wait' mean?" Samual asked.

"Alec was at work on the night shift. When he came home, he rang the police. They came, and I told them what I saw," Alice said.

"That's all from me, Your Honor," Jonathan said.

With an ace up her sleeve, Nancy said,

"I would like to call Edward Gilbert, Your Honor."

The clerk of the court swore Edward Gilbert in, and then Nancy asked,

"On the night of the murder, were you at the quay parked under the trees?"

"No, I know the spot; I have never parked there in my life; I was with my wife at a bingo meeting," Edward answered.

"Do you know Alice Jones?" Nancy asked.

"Yes, we are nodding acquaintances around the neighborhood," Edward said.

Jonathan rose with, "Your Honor, I would like to call Noelene Gilbert."

Edward Gilbert paled to a shade of gray when Noelene Gilbert was sworn in.

Jonathan's ace of hearts v. Nancy's ace of clubs.

"Mrs. Gilbert, can you identify your husband?"

"Yes, that's him sitting there." She pointed to Edward Gilbert.

"Where were you on the night in question?" Samual asked.

"I was playing bingo at the church hall," Noelene said.

"Was your husband with you?" Samual asked.

"No, I don't know where he was; I never do; I went with my next-door neighbor, Lily. I always play with her," Noelene answered.

"That completes our testimony, Your Honor," Samual said and sat.

"If there are no more last-minute statements, could the advocates complete the proceedings?" the judge said.

The advocates gave their closing statements to the jury.

The judge ordered the jury to their room to discuss the evidence and make their decision: guilty, not guilty, or not proven.

"We will have a break now and resume after the jury decides. Mr. Gilbert, I am placing you under arrest for perjury," the judge said.

All filed out of the court into the lobby except the accused, Gilbert, and the jury.

Justin approached Jonathan. "How did we go?"

"We were all right till Alice Jones, one hell of a tough lady, put her family life in jeopardy to tell what she saw, and the jury believed her. That fool Gilbert is in a lot of trouble. As for the judgment?"

He looked to the heavens and gestured with his hands.

"Either way."

It was a long break before the jury came back with a disputed verdict.

"We find the defendant guilty with a majority of seventeen votes. Seven votes were not guilty, and one not proven," the foreman stated.

As it is late, I will adjourn the matter until tomorrow for sentencing; this session is now closed," the judge said.

At first, the Wotans and others did not understand what all that meant, and confusion reigned. Heated discussion raged in the foyer for some time after.

Justin planned to visit Claire in the court holding cell. They directed him to an area of what seemed a small apartment.

"Of course, these cells are for not-guilty people, not only for guilty people," Justin reasoned.

Claire was ecstatic at seeing him and rushed into his arms.

"Justin, oh Justin," she said and burst into uncontrolled tears. "What is going to happen to me?"

He stood still until Claire settled.

"We won't know until the judge returns. It is his call. I am sure he will consider Wotan's ways and laws. In this place, things look fine and dandy. Are you nice and comfy? I want you to get one thing clear in your mind. You could go to prison," Justin said.

"That will kill me!" Claire cried.

"It won't, you know," Justin said.

"If I am going to prison, what will it be like?" Claire asked.

"Unlike those trash television shows, there are places that are like a holiday stay, but let's not get too far ahead of ourselves; we will wait until the judge gives the sentence tomorrow," Justin said.

She's brightened up a bit and accepted it.

Tomorrow came, and all the players returned, to the court at 10:00 a.m.,. Judge Anthony made his accepted method of entry, and after His Lordship sat, so did the crowd.

"On the matter of the guilty verdict in *The Crown versus Claire Wotan*, there has been much research and thought on sentencing, taking into consideration the unwritten laws of Wotan. As a starting point, Anna Burgess is dead, and we must accept the verdict. I would ask Claire Wotan to step forward." The judge then said,

"I sentence you to five years of internment, with a non-parole period of two years, at the Lilac Center in Glasgow."

Claire stood and looked as though the world's weight was on her shoulders.

"All stand," the clerk said.

All stood, and the judge, in all his regalia, left the courtroom.

"That's that?" Justin said to Jonathan.

"Afraid so. We could appeal, but we could finish worse than ever. Anthony was very lenient. He gave a lot of thought to Wotan law, sentencing, and internment," Samual said.

"Do you know of this Lilac Center?" Justin asked.

I haven't. It is new, but it is first class, specializing in rehabilitating," Samual said.

It took three days before Justin could visit. His visit had to have the approval of Claire and her supervisor. Unwanted males need not apply.

Chapter 12

The Lilac Center at Glasgow surprised Justin when he arrived. It was a pleasant building in a well-grassed area, with no wires or bars or anything to suggest a prison. He wandered up to the front door and rang the bell. A pleasant middle-aged woman answered the door and asked his name. She ticked him off her visitors' sheet and said,

"You are here to visit Claire Wotan. Do come in. It's not as if we dislike men, but we get undesirable partners knocking on the door from time to time," she said.

She unlocked another door.

"We are a correctional institution," she said and took him down a hall and knocked on a door. The door opened, and the biggest smile greeted him.

"Justin, Justin, hug me," Claire said.

When she settled down, Justin said, "Show me around the place." Which she did. It impressed Justin with the layout and newness of it all.

"This is a bit of all right; what do you think?" he said.

'It is like a holiday camp; everyone must be doing something, and there is no such thing as lounging around all day; they gave me a little booklet with everything in it. We'll return to my room, and I will show you," Claire said.

When they returned, Claire made Justin a cup of tea. "Here is that little booklet. Have a look and see what's in it for me."

Justin fingered through the booklet. "This is great. It's what you needed. Your life has been going nowhere, directionless. This place will give you a purpose. I want you to examine it and choose a career in your life. You were a smart young girl at school, and you knew where you were going. Get that direction back in your life now. As Mr. Nike says, 'Just do it.'"

"Yes, sir." She gave him a flicking salute.

"I am a bit of a bully, but you need my direction now; you have lost your confidence after that bastard Godley messed with your life. Here is the opportunity to get going again. This booklet they gave you is perfect," he said.

Justin examined the room and said, "How often could I come? Who do you want to see from Wotan? How about your mum and dad? I will drive them up. It would cheer them, and we could stay overnight," Justin suggested.

"Could you do that?" Claire asked.

"Yes, I could do that," Justin said.

"Well, I will find out from the staff when and where. It will relieve their worries and my guilt," Claire said.

She found out the where and when and phoned Justin.

"Next Monday," she said.

"Okay. I will organize things from the Wotan end; they were very excited when I told them. Your pa, with a twinkle in his eye, asked if he should bring his gun," Justin said with a laugh. Claire laughed as well.

"I don't know how well they will travel, so I will phone on the way and give you an ETA, as they say on the airlines," Justin said.

Monday arrived, and they were down at the wharf. *Esmeralda* was still operating on a holiday timetable and was to leave at 8:00 a.m. The three of them set off on their long trek. The sea was benign, and it was a pleasant journey to Kinlochbervie, where they disembarked and walked to Justin's car. The seat allocation was for Osgar to sit in the front with Justin, and Rhonda would have the whole backseat to herself.

Off they went; Justin figured the trip would take six hours, and they would arrive at Glasgow by midafternoon. That was his original hope, but it was not enough, they only got through the first hour before Rhonda wanted a stop.

"We should stop for tea, Justin," Rhonda said.

"Yes," conferred Osgar.

"That's all right, but we cannot be late for Claire, so after this, we go right through; oh, except for a petrol stop," Justin said.

"Roger and out," quipped Osgar. So they drove and arrived at the Lilac center by midafternoon. They ushered them into a guest lounge and Claire entered. Claire and her parents felt a shared excitement.

"Thanks again; I now know what growing up means," Claire said to Justin.

"Can we have a cup of tea, dear?" Rhonda asked.

"Good idea," said Osgar.

Justin wandered off to find someone or somewhere.

As they sat for tea, Claire spoke up.

"Justin, I have decided to study for a geriatric nursing qualification while here. My supervisor told me I could help as a volunteer at the nursing home down the road. They are always looking for staff. Good idea, aye?" Claire said.

"Great," said Justin.

"Then I could work with all the oldies at Wotan, such as Mum and Dad," Claire said.

"You have it all worked out. Good, good, good," Justin said.

Every few weeks, Justin, when he saw Claire, smiled at her friendly spirit and the increase in her confidence; she had found her place.

Back at Wotan, Dougal asked Justin about Claire.

"Ring the Lilac Center. Say what you want, and they will make an appointment," Justin said.

"I want to tell you something first; as you know, I was having a relationship with Anna and Claire at the same time. I thought this was very smart, and then Ma told me,

"If you keep burning the candle at both ends when you get to the middle, you will get burned. Mark my word, young man."

"Ma was right, and I am keen on Claire; what do I do now?" Dougal said.

"Holy moly, you young people get yourselves into strife. You caused all this death, trial, and jail business; do you know that?" Justin said.

"I do now," Dougal replied.

"The out is to look her in her eyes, tell her the truth, cop the blame, and ask for forgiveness. If she rejects you, keep going back. You can come with me next time I go up. Do you drive?"

"Yes, Pa says I'm a wonderful driver," Dougal said.

"Does he now? We will have to trust Dad. Let's see how you go," Justin replied.

In a fortnight, Justin left a message for Dougal, saying,

"Get the ferry over on Wednesday morning and meet me at Kinlochbervie wharf."

Dougal did as directed, and Justin drove clear of the traffic.

"Hop over, and you can drive; I won't talk about Claire and you or give any advice. Claire doesn't know you are coming. She will be glad to see you, but you must tell her your story, all of it, and see what happens," Justin said.

"All right," Dougal replied.

Dougal's driving was as good as his brag, and Justin let him drive to the outskirts of Glasgow.

"I'll drive now, Dougal; I know the shortcuts; we have made good time, and Claire will be waiting," Justin said.

The cleanness and space at Lilac impressed Dougal.

"Wow, do they call this a jail? It's more like home," Dougal said.

"Well, it's Claire's home at the moment; we'll have to see if we are welcome," Justin said as he parked.

They walked up to the front door, and the first signs of jail were a no-nonsense front door and an intercom camera overhead. A finger on a buzzer and a female voice answered.

"Pleased to see you, Mr. Abbott, and who is the unannounced guest accompanying you?" the voice answered.

"This is Dougal Wotan, one of Claire's special friends. I have brought him unannounced to see if the flame between them is still burning; I hope you don't mind," said Justin, addressing the camera.

"It is irregular, but do come in. I will have George let you in," the voice answered.

They passed through the first door and another door, which George opened. George was a middle-aged giant of a man whom no one crossed.

"Good day to you, Justin, is it? How are you traveling?" George asked.

"Like a rocket," Justin answered.

"Creditors after you?" George asked.

"Yes. If anyone comes in, tell them I caught a taxi out," Justin said.

"I'll do that, gov. You here to see Her Ladyship? She is in the library. I will take you to her," George said.

He ushered us into a small technical library. One person in a white jacket was present, who turned; it was Claire; she stood breathlessly still, her eyes locked on Dougal's eyes; dumbstruck, he stared back.

It was a moment, but it was as if time stood still. Dougal was the first to move as he enveloped Claire. She wrapped her arms around his waist. As their bodies intertwined, he looked down, and she looked up. Another pause, and then the kiss started. Both were unaware of Justin or George. They were the only two people in the world, and not one spoken word. It seemed forever when they separated and spoke sheepishly; silence followed.

"We'll get out of your hair and see you in the lounge," Justin said.

"Regulations," George said.

"George, we'll hear you in five minutes, and in five minutes, as you say, regulations," Justin uttered.

Although he looked like a lion, George was a lamb; he mumbled, "All right."

Justin and George left with a "see you in five minutes" and went to the lounge for coffee for Justin and tea for George.

Claire and Dougal sat and sat until Dougal said,

"Claire, I owe you an apology. My smartarse attitude caused all that trouble between you and Anna. I always wanted you. If I went out with Anna, you would be jealous and seek me out. Ma told me about burning the candle at both ends and how it would end in tears. She was right, you know. Forgive me for my foolishness."

Claire heard him out and thought it through. Her reply took time. Her response was measured, with a smile. "I hurt about what you've told me, Dougal, but that is behind us now. As your confessor, I will give you penance. You, Dougal, will see me weekly and bring me all the Wotan news, and any information you can find on geriatric care. I am studying nursing of older adults, to be useful to Wotan when I leave here."

"That's great, yes, I will do that, and as a bonus, I will throw in some kisses and cuddles," Dougal said.

"That's all? Kisses and cuddles?" Claire asked.

"No, it is not. Your wish will be my command," he replied.

Their five minutes were up, and they wandered across to the two men. Their entry was arm in arm, covered in smiles. Their smiles gave them away.

"Ha-ha, two Cheshire cats," Justin joked.

Dougal was true to his word and visited every week. He had brought so many books on care that she had to stop him. The reasons she and he treasured the visits were for the company and the extra covert activities that developed.

Claire was a trusted resident of the establishment and could handle the more difficult inmates, such as the drug withdrawal patients, who were after "stuff." The staff knew her nursing ambitions, and she was a Grade-A resident, and everyone trusted her, so much so that whenever the nursing home, a walk down the road, was short of staff, they would call the Lilac center and "borrow" Claire. Claire was keen on her studies and would go, now unescorted, to the oldies. She was learning medications, including opiates and injections, in her studies.

Claire's life cycle had settled. She had completed her competency skills at the nursing home and was now qualified to work anywhere. With Wotan contact through Justin, and regular contact with Dougal, life was as good as she could expect in prison. The supervisor summoned her to his office in her second year of internment.

"Claire, we have received some good news from the parole board. As of next Wednesday, which is the first of the month, your sentence is over; good behavior warranted this," the supervisor said.

Claire, instead of feeling elation, felt confusion.

"What about my patients? Many rely on me for conversation and help. I am their go-to lady," Claire pleaded.

"Yes, they may miss you, but you will find when you go back to Wotan, the old people will want you there, or you could take a position around here. You have myriad opportunities with your newfound skills; use them with wisdom. I have notified Mr. Abbott, and he will pick you up," the supervisor said.

They have kicked me out.

Chapter 13

Claire asked Justin to pick her up on the first of the month. Her demure manner surprised him. He drove a short distance in silence before pulling over.

"Oh-kay, tell me, what is it?" Justin queried.

Claire burst into tears, and Justin put his arm around her.

"They took all my patients and books; I've got nothing now," she cried.

"Nothing? You have a beautiful new future; Wotan, now full of old people, has been screaming for someone like you. We'll get back and sort out your new premises. Then you can do the rounds and meet all the old people. See Dr. Brodie, tell him of your training, show him your certificate, and inform him that you can administer tablets and injections. He will love it and appreciate a reduction in his workload."

As for how the people will accept you, no problems. You are a Wotan; under Wotan laws, you have done no wrong. You are a martyr. Come on, show a bit of confidence. It's all good. Dougal will meet us at the Kinlochbervie wharf and come back with us on *Esmeralda*. So, smarten yourself up," Justin said.

"That's what you say, but they are not all my friends, nor yours. Some say that we are living in sin," Claire said.

"I don't care what they say. We know the truth, and that's all that matters," Justin replied.

"How can I survive without you?" Claire said.

"Once you start your career in Wotan, the world is your oyster. You will regain your confidence," Justin said.

"Oysters, yuck," Claire said.

"Confidence, beautiful," Justin replied.

The rest of their drive was mundane, rather boring, and they were glad when they reached Kinlochbervie. Justin parked at Ted's Parking Place, and they gathered Claire's gear and headed to the wharf. Standing on the wharf was gangling Dougal with a giant smile; Claire reacted with her winning smile and rushed into Dougal's arms.

"How is the atmosphere for me up there?" Claire asked Dougal.

"Great, you're a local hero, punished by those outsiders and all," Dougal said.

The afternoon ferry arrived, and the trio boarded.

"How is the sea?" Justin asked a crew member. "Like a millpond," the man replied.

There was scant conversation on the trip, but Justin was aware of the nervous trepidation within Claire.

"Jolly up a bit, young lady. Everything will be fine," Justin said.

Dougal sat next to Claire, placed an arm around her shoulders, and she snuggled next to him. They completed the trip in silence. As they approached the wharf, there was a considerable crowd gathered.

"I hope they're not for me; I couldn't cope," Claire said.

"Come on, you will be all right," Justin said.

As they stepped onto the wharf, a group of her friends crowded around, and from the others gathered, there was polite clapping. Standing in the background were her ma and pa.

Claire rushed and hugged her mother.

"It's good to be back, Ma. Why all the people?" Claire asked.

"You are the first Wotan to have been inside. I should have shot one of the bastards," Pa said.

"You haven't still got that gun? Throw it away," Claire said.

"Never!" Pa replied.

Claire wandered through the crowd, thanking them for the welcome. Like all these things, it wound down until the core was the ones left.

Dougal said, "I'm going home; see you tomorrow." He left with a kiss to Claire and a handshake to Justin.

"I suppose we will go home to the house, and you can see the bachelor mess," Justin said.

"I hope not, remember? It's my house, but I must give deference to an older man," Claire answered with a smile.

They settled into the house and wrote a shopping list to pick up from the Kinlochbervie store tomorrow morning. They were up and ready to board when they met Dr. Brodie disembarking.

"Dr. Brodie," called Claire, "I must show you something right now."

"Claire, Justin, it's great to see you back," said the doctor.

There goes the shopping trip.

Claire took Dr. Brodie's arm and led him to the house, where she displayed her certificate showing all the units performed.

"Excellent, we need you here, but how did you perform the practical skills?" the doctor asked.

"At St. Agnes Nursing Home for the Aged, down the road from where I was," Claire said.

"Yes, I know it. Good establishment: they let you out, didn't they? You must have been a good girl," Doc said.

"The best," said Claire.

The die is cast.

'Do you have a gown? Put it on and we will do the rounds together," Doc said.

"Yes, I have, I will change," an excited Claire said.

Then Claire said to Justin, "I am sorry, Justin, but I had to take my chance."

"Go for it," Justin said; "we'll do the shopping tomorrow."

Claire was right into it, taking the temperature of the old, straightening bedrooms, administering tablets, and even giving an injection. She also knew most of the medications and their doses. One call was to a younger man with an infection in his leg.

"We will have to lance this, then drain it; we will get a lot of muck out of it," the doctor said. "You will have him come to you daily. Keep it clean and dressed for at least a week and keep the antibiotics up for a week. We must get a scab forming," the doctor said.

The doctor was very impressed by Claire's knowledge and work ethic.

"You will do well, young lady. I will be back next week unless you call me. I want everyone in Wotan to make you the point of call, and I will come over if you contact me," Dr. Brodie said.

Justin asked Dr. Brodie to fit in a time for a chat about wages and fees for Claire and whether she must upgrade her qualifications to apply for government funding.

The doctor came within a few days.

"We will need to apply for a distance learning qualification and apply for Claire to register as a district nurse; that will be difficult for her at Wotan. You know that politician fellow, George Hedley; put the squeeze on him," the doctor said.

"You are a learned fellow, and a genius as well. That's a brilliant idea. We control all the Wotan votes, and his seat is shaky. I will go to Aberdeen, to offer him again something he cannot refuse," said Justin gleefully.

Justin made the phone call and spoke to George Hedley's secretary about an appointment.

"Mr. Hedley is very busy at the moment; what's the call about?"

"Wotan," said Justin.

Justin heard a click, and a voice said, "Justin, it's been a long time. What can I do for you?"

"I need an urgent appointment about Wotan business. When can you fit me in?" Justin said.

"For you, how about tomorrow at two?" George said.

"Perfect. I will see you then," Justin replied.

Justin was down at the wharf to catch the ferry and drive to Aberdeen for his appointment with George Hedley. He received the political hail-fellow-well-met routine as soon as he arrived.

After all, we are the best of friends.

"How are you, Justin? You are looking well. What brings you here?" George said.

"Wotan brings me here, George."

"Wotan, aye. Step into my office and we will discuss your problems."

George's office was in a large room off his secretary's office.

We sat on either side of George's desk. "Tell me all," George said.

"We have a young lady named Claire at Wotan, who has a geriatric nursing certificate, and our number of aged residents is on the increase. We want her to be the Wotan nurse to service all the old people we have there. Also, we want part of an old house to be her treatment rooms, two or three rooms at the most. And most of all, we want the government to pay for it all," Justin concluded.

"Is that the young lady in all the newspapers?" George asked.

"Yes, she went to prison. That's where she received her training. She is keen to do this," Justin said.

"It shouldn't be too difficult; they are always looking for ways to service these remote locations, and you have a good start with a nurse and some premises. I will speak to my associate in the Health Department and see what we can do. Give me a ring in a few days, and I should have something sorted for you," George said.

George was true to his word. He rang Justin back at his office and left a message.

Chapter 14

"Justin, contact the director of nursing at Aberdeen Health Services and arrange an inspection. Pick the inspector up, take her to Wotan, and fix it up with her. You're at the mercy of the bureaucrats now. Good luck: let me know what happens," George Hedley said.

Being at his office in Edinburgh, he rang Aberdeen Health Services and spoke to the director of nursing to arrange the Wotan visit. The director put him through to Judith Kennedy, to arrange the visit to Wotan.

"Judy speaking," a pleasant female voice answered.

"Judy, my name is Justin Abbott from Wotan; I am to take you to assess the premises at Wotan as being suitable for the aged."

"Oh, yes, I received an email from the boss about this. You are lucky. I have a few days available now. How about tomorrow?" Judy said.

"That's perfect. I expected a long delay. I will pick you up. Where?" Justin asked.

"I assume you want an early start; how about my place, Unit two, Number four, O'Connell Place? It's right in town near the university." Judy said.

"I will find it. I'll see you at about eight in the morning. We have a long way to go," Justin replied.

The next morning, Justin was at the address before eight. It was an apartment on the ground floor of an old building; the door was open, so he called; "Judy."
A tall, well-proportioned, dark-haired lady in her mid-thirties answered.

"You're Justin, I presume; I will be ready in a sec. Will I be staying overnight?"

"Yes, it's a long drive," Justin said.

"Won't be a moment. I must ask Mrs. Hobbs, next door, to feed the cat," Judy said.

"Want me to carry anything?" Justin asked.

"Oh, I am sorry, come in, come in. There is hot coffee there," she said as she pointed at the coffee, then disappeared out the back to see Mrs. Hobbs.

"It's a big place. For one?" Justin asked.

"I have broken off with him; I am looking for someone else; you don't want a room, do you?" She laughed.

"Not at the moment; too much going on," Justin replied.

"Not depriving ourselves of life's essentials, are we?" she asked.

"Could be," Justin replied.

This will be a lively trip.

Judy took enough to fill the trunk of Justin's car, and then they were ready for the road.

"Do you know where we are going?" Judy said.

Justin pulled out the road map, unfolded it, and pointed to the location of Wotan.

"Way up there, there is nothing; the map is vacant," Judy said.

"Well, that's where we are going, to Scotland's end. The towns are too small for the map people to worry about," Justin said.

"You know you are responsible for my well-being?" she said as she put her hand on his leg.

Things have started, so I will play ball with you, lady.

"You can rely on me," he said.

"Oh, I do hope so,"

"Well, let's hit the road," he said.

And hit the road they did. The conversation covered many subjects. Wotan; marital situation; children; partners; and double entendre, which was Judy's forte, was in the constant banter.

This is usually a man's game.

Hand on leg and mention of loins were part of "the game." Justin rolled along with it while it was going, but they settled and listened to the radio. It was lunchtime when they reached Inverness and stopped for tea and sandwiches at a small roadside diner. It was here that Justin decided.

Making love with Judy is not all bad; it could be all good.

"Judy, when we get to Wotan, there is no accommodation, so you can sleep at my abode, not only in my abode, but in my bed with me. How does that sound? Music to your ears?" Justin asked.

"Horizontal dancing?" Judy trilled.

"Of course!" Justin replied.

My sacrifice to the cause.

Martyr Justin leaned over to give her a peck on the cheek. Judy reacted with a tongue halfway down his throat.

"Settle, my dear, settle down; we still have some driving to do," Justin said.

"My juices are flowing," Judy replied.

"Well, bottle them till later; we don't want you to run out. By the way, you're the navigator; how far to go?" Justin changed the subject.

Judy unfurled Kinlochbervie on her road map.

"How do I spell it?" Judy asked.

"Kin-loch-ber-vie." Justin broke the word into syllables. Look for the most northeastern bay; we are heading for there," Justin said.

"Here?" She poked the map at Justin.

"That's about it; We are about there," Justin replied.

It took some eventful time, until the conversation dribbled away, that they were on the outskirts of Kinlochbervie. They drove in, and Justin parked in his usual place. They could see the ferry at the wharf, and they gathered Judy's bits and pieces and meandered over.

The wharf gang was finishing loading for the trip to Wotan.

They boarded and sat in what Justin described as good viewing seats. The seas were calm, and the motor's hum increased as *Esmeralda* chugged across the open sea.

"Do you live right out here?" Judy asked.

"No, not all the time. I have a place in Edinburgh," Justin answered.

The rest of the trip was small talk, and the trip seemed slow. Justin knew he would have to gear up his manner to maintain her interest.

Before they arrived at Wotan, he placed his arm around her, nibbled her earlobe, and said, "Tonight, when I say good night, I will mean 'Good night, Judy'!"

"Goody, you are a bit of a wordsmith, aren't you?"

"I want to keep your juices flowing," Justin said with a laugh.

"Oh, you're doing that, that's for sure," Judy said.

"We are coming into Wotan now. You are going back in time; look around and get the feel of the place," Justin said.

Esmeralda tied up at the wharf, and they disembarked. Justin told Judy a little of Wotan's history; she was very interested. They walked around the village until they came to Claire's house. "This is the biggest house in Wotan and belongs to our nurse, Claire. All her patients that are still here are old people. She does her work for nothing. She's not here now. Step inside; this room is Claire's office; she works under the guidance of Dr. Brodie, who comes here once or twice a week from Kinlochbervie. She has it set up perfectly. I have the run of the house and have moved my rooms upstairs; come, and I will show you," Justin said.

They went upstairs to Justin's two rooms. "That's my room, and through the adjoining door is the other. The bathroom is down the hall. Nobody comes up here, so it's private, isn't it?"

"Yes, it is private," she said.

Justin cuddled her. "Tonight is closing in, yummy," he said.

"We must be downstairs when Claire gets in, so I can introduce you," Justin added.

Claire rushed in, saying, "I must see the doctor; Janie has had a turn. The boat is still at the wharf, so he will be here somewhere," as she headed out the door.

"Well, what do you say? That's Claire," Justin said to Judy.

"Busy girl," said Judy.

"I caught him," Claire said as she entered the room.

"Good work; now let me introduce you to Judy Kennedy from Aberdeen Health Service; she is here to look at the health services here at Wotan," Justin said.

"Hello, Judy. What can I tell you or show you?" Claire said.

"I don't want to show or tell you anything; I am here to ask what you need and what paperwork you need to get financial help from us. We will find a quiet place and chat," Judy said.

"Okay. How about here and now?" Claire said.

Judy looked at Justin, who replied,

"Why not? Right here at the table, I'll buzz off and leave you to it."

Judy went for her briefcase, and Claire collected an A4 writing pad. They cleared the kitchen table and went to work. Judy had a plethora of forms and time sheets, which she presented and explained to Claire. Overwhelmed, Claire worked her way through them.

"We need you to keep them and send them to us monthly, and on receipt, we will pay into your account the stipend, which means money, quite an amount. Now your patients, those without it, must apply for social services and a pension. The forms are in that big folder; go through everything, and if you get into a knot, ring me," Judy said.

Justin returned. "I've given Claire tasks to do," Judy said. "When she does, the money will start flowing."

"As a celebration," Justin said, "I will go to the wharf to get some fish for dinner, and we will need a bottle of good vino. Coming for a walk, Judy?"

"Love it," she replied as she took Justin's hand.

"Wotan is a pleasant place; I like it." Judy added.

"Most young people don't think so; they buzz off to the big cities."

"Why are you still here?" Judy asked.

"I am a schoolteacher; I work at the school, and I also do research on ancient tribes," Justin explained.

"Here?" Judy asked.

"The Wotans are descendants of ancient Celts who came from Gaul in Spain thousands of years ago. They have been here forever with scant interaction with other people. In the early years, nobody came here; it was too inhospitable," Justin said.

"Religion was the first to discover them; various groups came to convert them, most of them Christian. Last century, the bureaucrats found them and taxed them; from there, they dragged them into modern times," Justin said.

"You know all about them, professor?" Judy said.

"A fair bit," he replied. "Here is the fish. Can you cook?" Justin said.

"When my microwave is working, I am an expert in reheating frozen meals," Judy said.

"Well, I will do it. You can help me, and I will show you how."

"Hey, Donald, what basket are the big fish in?" Justin asked.

"I will get you one, sir," Donald said.

"The king has knighted you?" Judy asked.

"One of my old school students," Justin said.

"We'll go to Beryl McNabb's store and buy a nice bottle of white wine to go with our meal. Your choice, Judy. There's not a big choice here, but there are some nice ones."

Judy and Claire cooked, and Justin and Dougal set the tables. It was the most enjoyable evening, but Judy and Justin knew the night to come. Their exaggerated closeness showed every one of their needs, much to Claire's chagrin.

Justin was aware of Claire's edginess, but nobody else noticed it.

Give me space, Claire; you don't own me.

Justin was glad when the meal was over, and they went their various ways.

Claire said, "I am going to Dougal's place to play chess; I won't be long."

"Well, don't wake us when you come home," Justin said.

The couple left, and Judy and Justin were alone.

"Well, madam, I will escort you to your room," Justin said to Judy.

"Please do, squire," excited, Judy replied.

"I am having a shower; then you can come and join me. We'll get the travel dust off, and then who knows what?" Judy said.

"I can't wait to get my hands on you," Justin said.

"Start now," Judy whispered in his ear.

It started in the shower and ended in the bedroom. It was a blue night, deep blue with knobs on. God knows what time it was when they went to sleep. They were both spent when they dropped into a slumber of bliss.

"Well, thanks for that, madam. You warmed the cockles of my heart," Justin said to Judy when they awoke.

"Well, old chap, my cockles are red hot with satisfaction. That's something I don't get a lot of these days. I was dying from frustration until you came along. I thought you came from Heaven. Oh, didn't I give you a come-on?" Judy said.

"At first, you scared the living daylights out of me, but I adapted," Justin said.

They laughed, the laughter of friends.

"Ronald Reagan, when he was president of the USA, said,

"When a public servant says, 'I am from the government; and I'm here to help you,' shiver in fear. But that's not true; you have been a most helpful person, and I am biased, but you have a beautiful personality and"—he paused—"a yummy body."

Judy laughed. "You say that to get what you want; well, I am telling you, I will give it to you," she said.

"How could I not love you? There, I have said it," Justin said with a smile.

"You couldn't not love me," said Judy, giving Justin a peck on the cheek.

It took Claire a few months to become used to the new system, but the entire organization took a more professional look at the new office and rooms. The most significant change to Claire's life was her new income, paid into her new bank account at Kinlochbervie. To her, it was avarice. She did not know what to do with it; she became the village's soft touch. All and sundry were at her all the time.

Claire had become a serious, circumspect young woman. The fun of youth had now vanished. Justin was worried and sat her down for a chat.

"I'm having trouble getting Myor out of my mind. That shocked look on his face when I dropped the harrow. I should have faced the music. Instead, you got me off. I knew that I had done wrong, and it will not go away!" Claire said.

"Claire, I've let you blame me or others for too long. It's about time you started looking at yourself because you own your actions! Blaming your tribal dictates, or me, and don't forget that unwritten thousand-year-old rule book is so much poppycock."

Chapter 15

Claire completed all her tasks and was a businesslike lady around the village. Since Judy moved into Wotan, Claire felt not needed. She had thoughts that Justin would be hers. Now she had the burden of Myor's death, and not been the center of Justin's attention. He now focused on Judy instead of her. All this led to its logical conclusion: depression, deep depression. Doc Brodie was first to notice it and prescribed Prozac. Justin, in his masculine way, thought it mild blues that she would snap out of once Judy assimilated it into her life. Justin was wrong, very wrong.

It was during a medical audit that Doc Brodie noticed the abnormality. Two vials of fentanyl he prescribed for Mr. Bull, who had terminal cancer of the abdomen, were missing.

Claire? I hope she is not on that stuff. Why does she want that?

Claire had neglected her own well-being. She had a niggle in her left abdomen that she ignored. It went on and on, getting worse and worse, until she mentioned it to Doc Brodie.

"Is this why you took the Fentanyl? I despair with you professional people, neglect yourselves but care for others. Hop up on the exam table and let me feel it," Doc Brodie said.

Claire complied with his command.

"My God, girl, your tummy's hot on the right side, and it's swollen. You've got a ruptured appendix. You're an emergency," Dr. Brodie said and rang the wharf.

He spoke to the harbormaster.

"Where is *Esmeralda?*" Doc asked.

"Left Wotan a few minutes ago," the harbormaster said.

"Well, get it back; we have a sick woman, the nurse Claire," the doctor said.

"Strewth, Claire, is she all right?" the harbormaster said.

"She will be dead if you don't hurry," Doc said.

"It's done; it's on the way back at full bore," the harbormaster said.

"Call Dougal, tell him to get some muscle men to carry the bed to the boat," Doc said to Dobber, who was sniffing about.

"Consider it done, Doc," Dobber replied.

Claire's pain was so excruciating that the doctor gave her a pain-killing injection. "I don't enjoy doing this before anesthetics with all that stuff already in you," he said.

The town was abuzz with the news about Claire and the calling of the boat back; this had never occurred before. Claire and her entourage were aboard as soon as the boat came in.

"I will get an ambulance as soon as we get in range. I hope there is one around that we can use."

"Can't this boat go faster?" Doc said to the crew member.

"*Esmeralda* is doing about twelve knots instead of the usual seven or eight; I hope she doesn't blow," said the crew member.

Doc was on the phone as the boat approached Kinlochbervie.

"We're in good luck. There is an ambulance nearby that we can get. It will be at the wharf, waiting.

As they arrived, the ambulance was on the wharf. They transferred Claire to the ambulance gurney for the trip to Raigmore Hospital at Inverness; Dr. Brodie and Dougal accompanied her, promising they would keep her father sitting in the front seat, pacified. The night was pitch black, and drizzle was falling, meaning a slow trip to

Inverness. Claire's restlessness, nausea, and vomiting had subsided, but she was still, too still. Dr. Brodie worked at keeping Claire awake, talking to her as he had his stethoscope to her chest.

"What medical equipment do you have with you?" Doc asked the assistant.

"We have the heart paddles, oxygen, and a drip," replied the assistant.

"Give me an oxygen mask and set up that drip with saline. How long to go?" Doc asked.

"In this weather, about another two hours," answered the assistant.

"Tell your driver to radio Raigmore and tell them our ETA and say one word: peritonitis."

"Come here, Dougal, hold her hand and keep talking to her, speak of good things, even if you think she's not listening: no crying, hear me!" the doctor ordered.

Ashen-faced, Dougal performed his task. He told her of their dreams, keeping it going for the entire trip.

"Claire's heart is still beating. While there's life, there's hope," Doc said.

Between the doctor and Dougal, they kept at Claire until they arrived with the siren blaring. They were ready at the Emergency Department of Raigmore District Hospital. White-garmented staff swarmed around them, removing the gurney with Claire, and rushing her into the Emergency Department, where other white-garmented staff wheeled her behind curtains.

"They'll use keyhole surgery to drain her side, then the course of action is highfalutin, intravenous antibiotics. If that does not work, in she goes," Doc said, pointing to the doors saying SURGERY. "Then the infernal wait," Doc Brodie said.

The hospital staff shepherded them into a little private lounge.

"Osgar, you can take the settee and have a little snooze; we'll wake you if anything comes up. Me? I will nap in this chair. You'll need some sleep, Dougal; we don't know when they will want us again."

"What about Justin? Irrespective of the hour, he will want to know," Dougal said.

"If you have his phone number, call him," the doctor said.

Justin was half awake when he answered, "Who? Dougal, do you know the time?"

Dougal replied, "Claire's in hospital serious sick, touch-and-go. She is in Raigmore at Inverness."

"What happened? It doesn't matter; I am coming there," Justin said.

"He is coming down," Dougal said to Doc Brodie.

It was dawn when Justin arrived at the hospital and spoke to the night receptionist.

"Claire Wotan?" asked Justin.

The receptionist passed the call on. "Dr. Kavanah will be right down."

Dr. Kavanah was a white-coated young man with the inevitable stethoscope around his shoulders.

"Your relationship?" he asked Justin.

"She's from Wotan; I am her carer," Justin answered.

"I was coming to tell her family. I am sorry to announce she has passed away," he said.

Justin crumbled to his knees, crying at the doctor's feet, "Oh, no. oh, no." he sobbed. His loud crying disturbed Dougal, who came out of the adjoining lounge and saw the doctor standing over the crying Justin; he knew.

Dougal placed an arm around Justin and started crying in grief. The happenings at his feet flabbergasted Dr. Kavanah. He looked at the receptionist in despair. She rang an alarm. Everyone came: Security; then Osgar and

Dr. Brodie led the charge, which included a senior doctor, who took control. Osgar joined the tearful two. Pandemonium was the order of the night. Dr. Kavanah slipped away, his work done.

The full light of day brought the glum group together.

The group confusion had changed Justin from male Banshee to group organizer.

Dr. Brodie volunteered to go to the mortuary, identify Claire, and tell the mortician to keep Claire's body until further notice.

"This funeral will be at the Wotan chapel, It will be a Wotan funeral, so the funeral director will have to take Claire's body to Wotan, via *Esmeralda*. It will be tricky, but I will sort it out," Justin said.

Justin loaded the doctor, Dougal, and Osgar, in his car and headed to the local funeral parlor, where he said,

"We all better go in; I don't know who they will need here.

A man in a dark mourning suit greeted them when they entered the funeral parlor.

"May I be of help?" he asked.

"A young lady passed away; she is in the mortuary at the hospital in Inverness," Justin said.

"We can handle that, sir," the mortician said.

"Ah, but that's not all; we need the body to go to Wotan for burial. There is a little kirk there."

"Wotan? That's via the Kinlochbervie ferry; I know it. We can handle that, but at considerable cost."

"By the way, my name's Kevin," the mortician said, handing a business card to Justin, who replied, "Here is my business card; I will pay a reasonable fee. Please email an invoice to my office. I want everything to be the best; I will notify the Reverend at Wotan."

The very best for you, my love.

The four of them hopped into Justin's car and headed off on the long drive home. During their coffee break, Justin rang Judy.

"She had passed away from peritonitis. We shed a river of tears, but I have settled and resolved to arrange the burial at Wotan."

"I am sorry for you, Jussy; she was like your daughter. How are you coping?" Judy asked.

"I was in a mess then, but I'm all right now. We are on our way to Wotan to break the news," Justin answered.

'I better organize a replacement for Claire to keep continuity in the systems. I am going to catch the bus to Kinlochbervie. Don't worry about meeting me, I will see you at the house or somewhere about. I am a big girl now. Reserve our bedroom and find out from Dougal, whom he wants to see when he gets there, and have them meet him at the wharf. He must be in a dreadful state," Judy said.

"I'll do that, Auntie Organizer," Justin said.

"Me! The organizer! What about you, smarty-pants?" Judy laughed, and Justin joined her.

Before they left, Justin rang Dobber.

"Dobber, Claire passed away from peritonitis."

"Oh?" He understood 'passed away' but didn't understand 'peritonitis.'

Dobber, with the help of his mother and a dictionary, spread the word. The whole of Wotan was in shock. It was a rarity for one so young and valuable to go from them.

The group waited at Kinlochbervie for the mortician with Claire's coffin. They surprised Justin with the number of mortician helpers.

"We must get the coffin to the kirk. The transport from the ferry is the muscle of my helpers," the mortician explained as the group sat and waited for the ferry.

"It's only a little kirk. What if we can't get everyone inside?" Justin said.

"You should have mentioned it earlier. I'll see what I've got in the van," the mortician said, then yelled,

"Hey Charlie, is that outside projector in the van?!"

"Yes, boss."

"We'll take it with us," Then to Justin, "I'll fix it up."

"Thanks for that," Justin said.

"Does someone own a robust stepladder?" Kevin asked.

"Why? There is one at the kirk. They are always painting something," Justin replied.

"If we have a full house, rather than some missing out, we will have an outside broadcast," Kevin said.

"What about the burial?" Justin asked.

"What about it? That's another cost altogether."

Who should turn but Judy, who was aghast at Justin's plans?

After their initial greetings, Judy said,

"We're not going a tad too far with these arrangements, all these people," Judy swung her arm in an arc, "are we, Jussy?"

"No, love. Everything is in hand," Justin said.

Sure, but who's hand and for what?

Judy wandered about the settlement and said her hellos. During her rounds, she had a cup of tea and a chat with Osgar and Rhonda.

"It's been a sad and stressful time for everybody, and most of all, for you two. Tell me how you want the funeral to proceed," Judy said.

"We don't want it too big, a normal Wotan funeral service and burial. We've been around here for a long time, you know?" Rhonda said.

"That's the feeling I get. Now, it is Justin controlled and in danger of being bigger than *Ben-Hur*. I will have him come and speak to you. After all, you are her parents," Judy said.

Judy corralled Justin over a cup of coffee and a biscuit.

"I went for a walk around the village and had a cupper with Osgar and Rhonda. You should have a chat with them; see Rhonda. She runs the show," Judy said.

"Your wish is my command, fair lady. I've been meaning to do that," Justin said.

"I would like 'meaning to do' to be changed to 'meaning to do that now'! As soon as this cupper is over."

"Whoa, lady, I will do it now. Do you want to come?"

"I have the utmost faith in you, Jussy. Listen to what she has to say." Judy made an air kiss in his direction, and he smiled.

She has me wrapped around her little finger.

"Where is Claire's burial plot?" Justin asked the Reverend.

"It is last in the row. The gravediggers have finished it now for tomorrow's service. I have asked Osgar and Rhonda to be in the front next to Dougal. Would you and your wife like to be there?"

"Yes, that is what we wanted."

"It would be best if you say a few words. Nobody else is confident they can control their emotions," the Reverend said.

"That will be fine," Justin replied.

Nobody here can control their emotions. Why me?

It dawned a beautiful day for a funeral if there is such a thing.

True to estimations, the church, a simple-design weatherboard building that looked like a kirk, was to experience a full house for the first time in its history. Not only a full house, but an overflow.

"This is not because she is a Wotan, but because she had become Wotan's helper. Every old person in town will be here," Justin said.

The hour had come, and they saw flowers, radiant flowers at the church entrance. Then as they entered, before them, on its bier, centered in the aisle, Claire's expensive coffin. The overflow crowd had left the front pews to the family, Justin, and Judy. It was a somber Christian burial and many a handkerchief was in service. The Reverend asked if anybody would like to say a few words. Justin was the only volunteer.

He stood, and with an encouraging hand squeeze from Judy, moved forward and mounted the pulpit. He was silent for a moment, then fought his emotional tears before speaking without notes.

"I am a professional public speaker and have stood in front of a crowd, frequently, but on this occasion I have nothing to say except to express my emotions. You all feel the same about Claire, so I would like to go back to my personal association.

"I was, in my early days, a researcher on the history of man. At that stage, my then wife divorced me. I sought solace in the bottle and spiraled down to depression. I sought help. A friend told me as I was a respected schoolteacher, to start again as far away as possible as a teacher. Which turned out to be Wotan. Many of you here today, Claire's friends, will remember this. It was a setback. What did I find? A class of characterless zombies. Please forgive me if my comments offend you.

At heart, you were all lovable students. Why did I find this? Godley!

"One student stood out because she alone did not accept his ethos. Claire was rebellious. She debunked his religious teachings, stating man evolved.

"Remember Olivia?" pointing to a teary young woman, who nodded.

"As her teacher, I observed her progressive tendencies and her willingness to learn. She was only seventeen when her life collapsed. Godley's acolyte, Callach, found himself not even betrothed, but married to Claire. Did Claire or her parents have any say in it? No! No! No! Talk about going to Hell? This was worse."

He paused.

"Popular opinion was I'd seduced Claire. Scurrilous! Yes, I loved her, but as a father loves a daughter. We, Claire and I, would like that rumor closed."

"She also had the unfortunate death of Myor, her great friend. This happened because of her Wotan values, and then the encounter with No-Nonsense-Nancy, as you all know, was a hell.

All this did was give Claire a lot of unwanted publicity, but gladly final exoneration. But never forget the heartache she endured! Then there was the death of a non-Wotan woman that had Claire jailed. This gave Claire the opportunity to study geriatrics and work with the older Wotans who are here today.

Then it happened. We lost her. Taken away, as she was on the cusp of a normal adult life."

"Vale, Claire Jane Wotan. Rest in peace."

But instead of stepping down teary, Justin stood straight and tall and said,

"Claire was the Great Wotan Warrior of our times. She followed Wotan law to the letter, and suffered grievous consequences, and even jail, for all of you. You let Godley in!" he said as his voice quivered in anger.

As he spoke, his finger of shame swung in an arc and pointed at every adult in the room.

Justin was a mess when he sought the solace of Judy. He sat next to her and buried his face in her shoulder.

"Well, you have said it all. You have said what had to be said, and should have been said, right back to the time of Godley."

Unbeknownst to him, most of the adult Wotans felt the finger of shame point at them, and it took a few minutes for the emotions to settle.

Dougal and his hefty friends, following the Reverend, carried the casket up the little hill to the prepared burial site. The cemetery was vast. As Justin and Judy looked around, the Reverend explained,

"Justin and Judy, this place had been in use for generations upon generations. We are using the sites from the last century, so Claire will be among friends."

They gazed around the field of white crosses, all the same except for the inscriptions. Justin glanced at the prepared cross for Claire and read the inscription: "RIP, Claire Jane, Loving Daughter of Rhonda and Osgar."

They lowered the casket into the prepared site; a tearful moment, and the first shovelful of soil peppered the shiny new casket.

That's all we have, my love.

Justin wiped tears from his eyes as the casket disappeared under the soil, and the flock dissipated.

"That's added an epoch bookmark to your life. Life, it's still going on, I hope?" Judy looked hard at him.

"Yes, new times are coming. What was that you said, 'an epoch.'" Is that a start or a finish?"

"For a start with no finish, but on second thought, you will be a wrinkly old fuddy-duddy in fifty years' time; at that point, I would like to renegotiate," Judy said.

"You would put a smile on the face of Buster Keaton," Justin laughed.

Thanks for giving that shoulder to rest on. I am now starting a new phase of my life with my wife," he said, as he gave Judy a peck on the cheek. She replied with a quick cuddle.

They, and a few Wotans, tidied up the kirk and environs before Kevin and his entourage departed.

It took a while for Wotan to return to normal, the days passed, and the memories dimmed, and life went on.

Justin and Judy were enjoying a cupper when a letter arrived addressed to The Estate of Claire Jane Wotan.

"What do we do with this?" Justin asked Judy.

"Well, open it. Claire can't," Judy replied.

"It is from that solicitor in Kinlochbervie. It's Claire's will," Justin said.

"That should go to Dougal. He's staying at his parents' place now. I must see his mum about her knee. I will take it and go now," Judy said.

When Judy returned, she said,

"Guess what? She left everything to her husband, including this house, so Dougal is our landlord."

"It is not as bad as it seems. It is not freehold. In Wotan, all land is on one company title. I set it up. The shareholders must give their consent for a new owner. We could build a house behind this one if we must. It's nice there. Anyhow, we will speak to Dougal when he appears."

"I could live here. When I was a kid, I lived on a farm. It's nice and peaceful," Judy said.

When Dougal came in to see them, Justin was straight into him.

"How does Wotan fit into your plans?"

"I was about to start work with Mr. Brown at Kinlochbervie before all this Claire trauma. That is the first time I have said Claire's name without crying. I have decided on Pa's suggestion, to get stuck into my future, instead of moping around here. So that is what I am doing, "Dougal said.

"Good for you. You will do well, Dougal. Health will pay you to do some book for the old people here as well," Judy said.

"Where are you going to live?" Justin asked.

"Mr. Brown will give me a room for the time being. I will be over there in the immediate future. The ferry travel is too restrictive. I can't see me coming back."

"I like it here. I'll take your place on the list to keep the numbers up." Judy said.

"Judy wants to have a health center and clinic in this house. She is confident the health department will buy this property from you, so get an appraisal from an agent and they will buy you out."

Dougal wandered off and Justin pulled Judy to him and whispered in her ear, "I want to go to bed with you. I've got the feeling."

"Jussy, you darling. I will reciprocate your feeling with bells and whistles , just as long as you have paid all owing debts."

End

www.ingramcontent.com/pod-product-compliance
Lightning Source LLC
Chambersburg PA
CBHW051432290426
44109CB00016B/1529